MEDITERRANEAN
Diet Cookbook
FOR BEGINNERS:

Your Odyssey Book of Quick & Easy Recipes with Simple Ingredient Lists for Eating Well Every Day, Ideal for Busy Lives, 30-Day Meal Plan to Refresh Your Diet

By Casey Malcolm

All rights reserved worldwide.
No part of this book may be reproduced or transmitted in any form or by any means, electronic or mechanical, including photocopying, recording, or by any information storage and retrieval system, without written permission from the publisher, except for including brief quotations in a review.

Warning-Disclaimer
The purpose of this book is to educate and entertain. The author or publisher does not guarantee that anyone following the techniques, suggestions, tips, ideas, or strategies will become successful. The author and publisher shall have neither liability nor responsibility to anyone with respect to any loss or damage caused or alleged to be caused, directly or indirectly, by the information contained in this book.

Copyright© 2023 By Casey Malcolm

TABLE OF CONTENTS

Introduction: Why This Book is Your New Best Friend in the Kitchen 4

Why Go Mediterranean? 6

    - The Basics 6

    - Key Benefits 6

    - Core Ingredients 7

    - General Meal Planning Tips 8

Chapter 1: Swift Breakfasts to Beat the Clock 9

Chapter 2: Bite-Size Snacks for Those Micro-Breaks 18

Chapter 3: Dips and Sides to Jazz Up Your Main Course 26

Chapter 4: Lightning-Fast Lunches for the Office or Home 35

Chapter 5: Speedy Dinners So You Can Get On With Your Evening 45

Chapter 6: 5-Ingredient Wonders 55

Chapter 7: Satisfy That Sweet Tooth in Minutes 61

Chapter 8: Easy, Breezy Beverages 70

Chapter 9: 30-Day Meal Plan: Your Roadmap to Culinary Happiness 76

Chapter 10: FAQs and Cooking Hacks for the Kitchen Novice 79

Measurement Conversion Chart 82

Glossary for Beginners 83

Additional Resources:

    - Kitchen Tools Guide 84

    - Essential Pantry Items 84

    - Pairing Suggestions 85

    - Ingredient Substitutions 86

Index 87

INTRODUCTION

Hello there, culinary adventurer! If your idea of a «quick dinner» usually involves a microwave and a questionable frozen meal, you're in for a treat. No, seriously, put down that sad cardboard box. If you've ever been convinced that eating healthy is complicated or time-consuming—often both—I invite you to a paradigm shift.

PROBLEMS, PROBLEMS, PROBLEMS

I get it; you're juggling a thousand things at once. Between work, social commitments, and maybe even a gym visit or two (on a good week), the last thing you have time for is whipping up a 5-course gourmet meal every night. Even if you manage some basic cooking projects, I can hear you sigh at the thought of another bland chicken salad or the monotony of another week of meal-prepped stir-fry.

Maybe you've got dietary restrictions, picky eaters in the family, or a complex relationship with anything involving preheating an oven. You want to eat better, feel better, and maybe impress a date or two with your culinary prowess—but where on earth do you find the time or energy? Let's not even get started on those «easy recipes» that require exotic spices you can't pronounce and utensils you didn't know existed.

VOILÀ, YOUR SOLUTION!

Strap on your apron and prepare to be amazed. This cookbook—your new culinary bible—is all about infusing your life with delicious, wholesome, and, above all, *quick* Mediterranean meals. Don't let the «Mediterranean» part intimidate you; we're talking about simple, delicious food that you can prepare even on a manic Monday. From 5-minute salsa to 15-minute beef stir-fry, and yes, even Instant Pot Chicken Risotto, these recipes are designed for real people living in the real world with real-time constraints.

YOUR LIFE, BUT BETTER

Imagine being the sort of person who can whip up Instant Hummus & Veggies for a quick snack instead of reaching for a bag of greasy chips. Picture a world where you look forward to lunch, with options like Spicy Tuna Salad or Quick Shrimp Tacos instead of another round of fast-food roulette.

And yes, this transformation comes without having to spend three hours in the kitchen or having to earn a culinary degree. Plus, let's be honest, who wouldn't want to be the life of the party, dazzling guests with Whipped Feta and Olive Tapenade?

WHY LISTEN TO ME?

Now, you might wonder, why should you trust me, Casey Malcolm, on this culinary journey? Not to toot my own horn, but I've spent years researching, practicing, and teaching the art of quick and healthy cooking. My recipes have been kitchen-tested more times than I can count, often under the watchful eyes of the harshest critics: busy parents, skeptical teenagers, and even some die-hard fast-food aficionados. The goal has always been to make healthy eating as accessible and enjoyable as possible.

ONWARD TO FLAVOR TOWN

So, let's set sail! Our first stop is 'Bite-Size Snacks for Those Micro-Breaks.' Who said healthy snacks had to be boring or time-consuming?

Prepare to have your taste buds tickled, your grocery list simplified, and your mealtime stress reduced to zero. Yes, you can thank me later—preferably with a plate of Fast Falafel Wrap or Instant Green Smoothie in hand.

Ready? Set? Let's cook!

—Casey Malcolm

P.S. Don't forget to try the 3-Ingredient Cookies. You won't believe what the third ingredient is. But you'll have to read on to find out!
Let the feast begin!

WHY GO MEDITERRANEAN?

THE BASICS

You might wonder why the focus is on Mediterranean-inspired recipes in a book about quick, simple, and tasty meals. Well, the Mediterranean lifestyle offers more than just culinary pleasures—it's a proven roadmap for overall well-being. Yes, that's right: you get to eat fantastic food and feel amazing. This book is not a strict guide to the traditional Mediterranean diet but an adaptation that fits into our modern lives. We embrace the fundamental elements of this diet and offer them in a format that accommodates different dietary needs and time constraints.

KEY BENEFITS:

HEART HEALTH

The Mediterranean diet is renowned for its cardiovascular benefits, mainly due to the abundance of heart-healthy fats in ingredients like olive oil and the omega-3 fatty acids found in fish. Numerous studies indicate that adopting this diet has the potential to decrease the levels of harmful cholesterol in the body, which in turn can help reduce the likelihood of developing heart disease.

BALANCED DIET

You'll find an emphasis on fruits, vegetables, and whole grains, the cornerstones of a balanced diet. These foods provide essential nutrients, fiber, and antioxidants, contributing to a strong immune system and glowing skin.

LONGEVITY & MENTAL HEALTH

People in Mediterranean countries tend to live longer, healthier lives than in many other countries. It is well known that a natural, well-balanced diet has a good effect on mental health, including lowered chances of depression and cognitive decline.

FLEXIBILITY & INCLUSIVITY

While traditional Mediterranean cuisine can be varied, it also offers the flexibility to adapt to various dietary restrictions, including vegetarian, vegan, and gluten-free lifestyles.

ENJOYMENT & MINDFULNESS

Perhaps one of the most underrated aspects of the Mediterranean lifestyle is focusing on enjoying meals as social, pleasurable experiences. Eating is not just a mechanical necessity but an opportunity to slow down and savor life.

CORE INGREDIENTS

Here are some must-have items that are as versatile as they are nutritious. Keeping these in your kitchen will make it easier to whip up these quick Mediterranean delights.

Olive Oil: The heart and soul of Mediterranean cooking. olive oil contains healthy fat, is rich in antioxidants, and is beneficial for your heart.

Fresh Fruits and Vegetables: Stock up on leafy greens, bell peppers, tomatoes, and seasonal fruits like oranges and berries.

Whole Grains: Quinoa, whole-wheat pasta, and brown rice provide filling fiber and essential nutrients.

Seafood: Fatty fish like salmon, sardines, and mackerel are staples. They're chock-full of omega-3 fatty acids, which are good for your heart and brain.

Legumes: Chickpeas, lentils, and other pulses are protein-packed and highly versatile.

Herbs and Spices: Fresh or dried herbs like basil, oregano, rosemary, and spices like garlic and paprika add layers of flavor without many additional calories.

By combining these core ingredients with the convenience of modern cooking techniques, this cookbook gives you the best of both worlds: delicious, wholesome meals that you can prepare in a flash.

GENERAL MEAL PLANNING TIPS

Portion Control: It's essential to tailor your portion sizes based on specific calorie and macronutrient requirements.

Leftovers: Some meals, like the One-Pot Mediterranean Chicken or Instant Pot Pulled Pork, may produce leftovers that you can use for another meal.

Meal Prepping: Consider prepping veggies and meats on a weekend to make your 10 – 15-minute meals quicker during the weekdays.

Substitutions: Feel free to substitute ingredients based on personal dietary restrictions or preferences.

Nutritional Info: If you can, calculate the nutritional information for each meal to ensure you're meeting your dietary goals.

Thematic Days: You could consider having thematic days like «Fish Fridays» or «Meatless Mondays» to introduce a more systematic approach to diversity in your diet.

Tailoring Your Breakfast to Your Day: Even amidst a busy schedule, aligning your breakfast choice with the day's demands can be brilliant. A carb-rich breakfast could provide energy if your day involves physical activity or a long stretch before lunch. On a more sedate or relaxed day, a protein-rich breakfast may be a better fit, aiding in muscle maintenance and providing a steady release of energy.

Seasonal Produce: Utilize seasonal fruits and vegetables to add freshness and variety and save on costs.

Supplements: If you're lacking in specific nutrients, consider supplementing wisely. However, consult a healthcare provider for personalized advice.

Professional Consultation: If you're looking for personalized suggestions, a consultation with a registered dietitian could be beneficial to ensure your meal plan is aligned with your health goals.

Remember, this meal plan is just a guide. Feel free to adjust based on your lifestyle, nutritional needs, and any medical conditions you may have.

Welcome to your Mediterranean lifestyle, adapted for the hustle and bustle of today's world. Happy cooking!

CHAPTER 1:
SWIFT BREAKFASTS TO BEAT THE CLOCK

Let's face it: mornings can be tough. Whether you've snoozed your alarm one too many times or are just trying to get the kids out the door, breakfast often takes a back seat. But fear not. This chapter is about solving that time crunch without sacrificing your taste buds or waistline.

OVERNIGHT OATS: ASSEMBLE & FORGET

4 Serves | **5** min Prep. | **0** min Cook* | Complexity

* (it's overnight; you can thank me later)

INGREDIENTS
- 1 cup rolled oats
- 2 cups almond milk
- 1 banana, sliced
- 1 tablespoon chia seeds
- 1 teaspoon honey
- 1/2 teaspoon cinnamon

DIRECTIONS
Combine oats, almond milk, banana, chia seeds, honey, and cinnamon in a large bowl.
Pour the mixture into jars, seal, and refrigerate overnight.
Give it a good stir in the morning and enjoy it cold or warm.

NUTRITIONAL INFORMATION: 240 calories | 6g protein | 32g carbs | 8g fat, 6g fiber | 0mg cholesterol | 80mg sodium | 180mg potassium.

QUICK TIP: Remember, oats expand, so leave a little room at the top of your jar.

DID YOU KNOW? Oats are a great source of fiber and can help you manage your weight. Now, who said being healthy had to be boring?

5-MINUTE SMOOTHIE BOWL

2 Serves | **5** min Prep. | **0** min Cook | Complexity

INGREDIENTS
- 1 cup frozen mixed berries
- 1 banana
- 1/2 cup Greek yogurt
- 1/2 cup almond milk
- Toppings: sliced almonds, chia seeds, coconut flakes

DIRECTIONS
Blend the mixed berries, banana, Greek yogurt, and almond milk until smooth.
Serve in bowls and sprinkle with desired toppings like sliced almonds, chia seeds, and coconut flakes.

NUTRITIONAL INFORMATION: 200 calories | 7g protein | 34g carbs | 5g fat | 7g fiber | 3mg cholesterol | 55mg sodium | 250mg potassium.

QUICK TIP: Always have a stash of frozen berries in the freezer for a last-minute smoothie bowl fix!

DID YOU KNOW? Greek yogurt is rich in protein and calcium, making your bones and muscles say, «Thank you!»

Chapter 1: Swift Breakfasts to Beat the Clock

QUICK BREAKFAST TACOS

4 Serves | 10 min Prep. | 5 min Cook | Complexity

INGREDIENTS
- 4 small corn tortillas
- 4 eggs, scrambled
- 1/2 cup diced tomatoes
- 1/4 cup diced onions
- 1 avocado, sliced
- 1/4 cup fresh cilantro, chopped
- Salsa, to taste

DIRECTIONS
Heat tortillas on a dry skillet over medium heat until warm and slightly crispy.
In another skillet, scramble the eggs to your liking.
Assemble tacos by layering eggs, diced tomatoes, onions, avocado slices, and cilantro.
Drizzle salsa on top for extra zing!

NUTRITIONAL INFORMATION: 320 calories | 12g protein | 29g carbs | 19g fat | 8g fiber | 180mg cholesterol | 250mg sodium | 400mg potassium.

QUICK TIP: Use pre-diced frozen onions to save on prep time.

DID YOU KNOW? Avocado is not just trendy; it's loaded with heart-healthy fats.

GREEK YOGURT WITH HONEY & WALNUTS

2 Serves | 3 min Prep. | 0 min Cook | Complexity

INGREDIENTS
- 1 cup Greek yogurt
- 2 tablespoons honey
- 1/4 cup walnuts, roughly chopped

DIRECTIONS
Spoon Greek yogurt into bowls.
Drizzle honey over the yogurt.
Sprinkle walnuts on top and give it a gentle stir if you like.

NUTRITIONAL INFORMATION: 220 calories | 12g protein, 20g carbs | 11g fat | 1g fiber | 5mg cholesterol | 40mg sodium | 120mg potassium.

QUICK TIP: Customize with seasonal fruits for added flavor and nutrition.

DID YOU KNOW? Walnuts are a great source of Omega-3 fatty acids, excellent for your brain health!

AVOCADO & TOMATO TOAST

2 Serves | 5 min Prep. | 2 min Cook | Complexity ★★☆☆☆

INGREDIENTS
- 2 slices whole-grain bread
- 1 avocado, peeled and pitted
- 1 medium tomato, sliced
- Salt and pepper, to taste

DIRECTIONS
Toast the bread to achieve your desired crunch.
Mash the avocado and evenly spread it over the toasted bread.
Layer the tomato slices on top.
Season with salt and pepper to taste.

NUTRITIONAL INFORMATION: 280 calories | 6g protein | 28g carbs | 18g fat | 8g fiber | 0mg cholesterol | 150mg sodium | 450mg potassium.

QUICK TIP: Add a poached egg on top for a protein boost!

DID YOU KNOW? Tomatoes are rich in antioxidants, particularly lycopene, which is good for your heart.

MICROWAVE VEGGIE OMELET

1 Serves | 3 min Prep. | 2 min Cook | Complexity ★☆☆☆☆

INGREDIENTS
- 2 eggs
- 1/4 cup bell peppers, diced
- 1/4 cup spinach, chopped
- Salt and pepper, to taste

DIRECTIONS
In a microwave-safe mug, whisk the eggs.
Add the bell peppers and spinach; stir to mix.
Microwave on high for 2 minutes or until eggs are fully cooked.

NUTRITIONAL INFORMATION: 180 calories | 14g protein | 4g carbs | 12g fat | 1g fiber | 370mg cholesterol | 120mg sodium | 200mg potassium.

QUICK TIP: Keep pre-chopped veggies in the fridge for an even faster breakfast prep!

DID YOU KNOW? Spinach is packed with iron and helps improve eye health!

Chapter 1: Swift Breakfasts to Beat the Clock

QUINOA PORRIDGE

4 Serves | **5** min Prep. | **15** min Cook | ★★☆☆☆ Complexity

INGREDIENTS
- 1 cup quinoa, rinsed
- 2 cups almond milk
- 1 tablespoon honey
- 1 teaspoon vanilla extract
- 1/4 teaspoon cinnamon
- A pinch of salt
- Fresh berries for garnish

DIRECTIONS
Combine quinoa and almond milk in a saucepan and bring to a boil.
Lower the heat, add honey, vanilla, cinnamon, and salt. Stir well.
Simmer for approximately 15 minutes, stirring now and then, until the quinoa becomes soft.
Serve hot, garnished with fresh berries.

NUTRITIONAL INFORMATION: 210 calories | 6g protein | 37g carbs | 4g fat | 3g fiber | 0mg cholesterol | 75mg sodium | 150mg potassium.

QUICK TIP: Almond milk can be switched to any other milk you enjoy.

DID YOU KNOW? Quinoa is actually a seed, not a grain, and it's a complete protein source!

SPEEDY SHAKSHUKA

2 Serves | **5** min Prep. | **10** min Cook | ★★★☆☆ Complexity

INGREDIENTS
- 1 tablespoon olive oil
- 1/2 onion, chopped
- 1 clove garlic, minced
- 1 can (14 oz) diced tomatoes
- 4 eggs
- Salt and pepper to taste
- Fresh parsley for garnish

DIRECTIONS
Heat olive oil in a pan, add onions and garlic and cook until they are translucent.
Add diced tomatoes and simmer for a few minutes.
Create small indentations in the tomato mixture and carefully place the eggs.
Cover the pan and let the eggs cook to your heart's content.
Add a pinch of salt and pepper, and finish with a sprinkling of parsley for garnish.

NUTRITIONAL INFORMATION: 270 calories | 13g protein | 14g carbs | 17g fat | 4g fiber | 370mg cholesterol | 440mg sodium | 400mg potassium.

QUICK TIP: Use a cast-iron skillet if you have one. It helps cook the eggs evenly!

DID YOU KNOW? Shakshuka originates from North Africa and is a popular breakfast dish in many Middle Eastern countries!

MUFFIN-TIN EGG BITES

6 Serves | **10** min Prep. | **20** min Cook | Complexity

INGREDIENTS
- 6 eggs
- 1/2 cup diced vegetables (e.g., bell peppers, mushrooms)
- 1/4 cup grated cheese (e.g., cheddar or feta)
- Salt and pepper to taste

DIRECTIONS
Preheat the oven to 375°F (190°C) and grease a muffin tin.
Take a bowl, blend the eggs smoothly, and mix in the diced vegetables and cheese, seasoning with salt and pepper.
Pour the mixture into the muffin tin.
Bake for 20 minutes or until the egg bites are fully cooked.

NUTRITIONAL INFORMATION: 270 calories, 20g protein | 4g carbs | 20g fat | 1g fiber | 325mg cholesterol | 220mg sodium | 180mg potassium.

QUICK TIP: These are perfect for meal prep; store in the fridge and reheat as needed!

BREAKFAST QUESADILLA

2 Serves | **5** min Prep. | **10** min Cook | Complexity

INGREDIENTS
- 2 tortillas
- 1/2 cup scrambled eggs
- 1/2 cup grated cheese
- 1/4 cup diced tomatoes
- 1/4 cup avocado slices

DIRECTIONS
Heat a non-stick pan over medium heat.
Place a tortilla in the pan, and add half of the cheese, scrambled eggs, tomatoes, and avocado slices.
Top with the remaining cheese and place the second tortilla on top.
Cook for 5 minutes per side or until the tortillas become crispy, and the cheese is melted.

NUTRITIONAL INFORMATION: 320 calories | 18g protein | 20g carbs | 20g fat | 3g fiber | 220mg cholesterol | 350mg sodium | 250mg potassium.

QUICK TIP: Add hot sauce or salsa for an extra kick!

BAGEL WITH SMOKED SALMON

2 Serves | 5 min Prep. | 0 min Cook | Complexity

INGREDIENTS
- 2 whole-grain bagels, halved
- 4 oz smoked salmon
- 1/4 cup cream cheese
- 1 tablespoon capers
- Fresh dill for garnish

DIRECTIONS
Toast the bagel halves until golden brown.
Spread cream cheese on each bagel half.
Place smoked salmon over the cream cheese.
Sprinkle capers and dill for garnish.

NUTRITIONAL INFORMATION: 300 calories | 20g protein | 30g carbs | 10g fat | 3g fiber | 25mg cholesterol | 600mg sodium | 150mg potassium.

QUICK TIP: Go light on the cream cheese to make it healthier, or opt for low-fat cream cheese!

INSTANT CHIA PUDDING

4 Serves | 5 min Prep. | 0 min Cook* | Complexity

* (requires 2 hours to set)

INGREDIENTS
- 1/4 cup chia seeds
- 1 cup almond milk
- 1 teaspoon vanilla extract
- 1 tablespoon honey

DIRECTIONS
Mix chia seeds, almond milk, vanilla extract, and honey in a bowl.
Pour the mixture into small jars or cups.
Refrigerate for at least 2 hours to let the pudding set.

NUTRITIONAL INFORMATION: 180 calories | 4g protein | 14g carbs | 8g fat | 7g fiber | 0mg cholesterol | 50mg sodium | 100mg potassium.

QUICK TIP: Use a cast-iron skillet if you have one. It helps cook the eggs evenly!

BANANA PANCAKES: FLIP & FLY

4 Serves | **10** min Prep. | **10** min Cook | Complexity ★★☆☆☆

INGREDIENTS
- 2 ripe bananas, mashed
- 1 cup all-purpose flour
- 1 teaspoon baking powder
- 1 egg
- 1/4 cup milk
- 1 tablespoon butter for greasing

DIRECTIONS
In a bowl, mix mashed bananas, flour, and baking powder.
Beat in the egg and milk to form a batter.
Heat a non-stick skillet and add a dab of butter.
Pour ladlefuls of batter and cook until bubbles show on top, then flip and cook the other side.

NUTRITIONAL INFORMATION: 220 calories | 5g protein | 40g carbs | 4g fat | 2g fiber | 55mg cholesterol | 200mg sodium | 300mg potassium.

QUICK TIP: Serve with fresh berries or a dollop of Greek yogurt for extra goodness!

QUICK & FILLING SMOOTHIES

2 Serves | **5** min Prep. | **0** min Cook | Complexity ★☆☆☆☆

INGREDIENTS
- 1 banana
- 1 cup frozen berries
- 1 cup spinach
- 1 cup almond milk
- 1 tablespoon chia seeds

DIRECTIONS
Combine all ingredients in a blender.
Blend until smooth.
Pour into glasses and serve immediately.

NUTRITIONAL INFORMATION: 180 calories | 3g protein | 32g carbs | 3g fat | 5g fiber | 0mg cholesterol | 100mg sodium | 400mg potassium.

QUICK TIP: Add a scoop of your favorite protein powder for a protein boost.

Chapter 1: Swift Breakfasts to Beat the Clock

ZUCCHINI & EGG BREAKFAST WRAP

2 Serves | **10 min** Prep. | **10 min** Cook | Complexity ★★☆☆☆

INGREDIENTS
- 2 whole-grain tortillas
- 1 small zucchini, thinly sliced
- 4 eggs, beaten
- 1/4 cup shredded cheese
- Salt and pepper to taste
- 1 tablespoon olive oil

DIRECTIONS
Warm the olive oil in a skillet and cook the zucchini until it softens.

Pour the prepared eggs into the skillet, add salt pepper, and softly scramble.

Spoon the egg-zucchini mixture onto tortillas. Sprinkle shredded cheese and roll up the tortillas.

NUTRITIONAL INFORMATION: 320 calories | 15g protein | 25g carbs | 16g fat | 3g fiber | 350mg cholesterol | 440mg sodium | 300mg potassium.

QUICK TIP: Add some salsa or hot sauce for an extra kick!

CHAPTER 2:
BITE-SIZE SNACKS FOR THOSE MICRO-BREAKS

Chapter 2: Bite-Size Snacks for Those Micro-Breaks

INSTANT HUMMUS & VEGGIES

4 Serves | 5 min Prep. | 0 min Cook | Complexity

INGREDIENTS
- 1 cup store-bought hummus
- 1 cup baby carrots
- 1 cup cucumber slices
- 1 cup bell pepper strips

DIRECTIONS
Arrange the veggies on a platter. Serve with hummus.

NUTRITIONAL INFORMATION: 150 calories | 5g protein | 20g carbs | 5g fat | 6g fiber | 0mg cholesterol | 300mg sodium | 200mg potassium.

QUICK TIP: You can also make your hummus if you're adventurous. Chickpeas, lemon juice, garlic, and tahini are all you need!

DID YOU KNOW? Avocado is not just trendy; it's loaded with heart-healthy fats.

CHEESE & CRACKER BITES

4 Serves | 5 min Prep. | 0 min Cook | Complexity

INGREDIENTS
- 20 crackers
- 20 small slices of cheddar cheese

DIRECTIONS
Place a cheese slice on every cracker. Serve instantly, or if planning for later, stash them in an airtight container.

NUTRITIONAL INFORMATION: 170 calories | 8g protein | 15g carbs | 10g fat | 0g fiber | 20mg cholesterol | 400mg sodium | 50mg potassium.

QUICK TIP: Jazz it up with olives or cherry tomatoes on top!

QUICK TRAIL MIX

4 Serves | **5 min** Prep. | **0 min** Cook | Complexity ★☆☆☆☆

INGREDIENTS
- 1 cup mixed nuts
- 1/2 cup dried fruit
- 1/4 cup chocolate chips

DIRECTIONS
Combine all ingredients in a large bowl. Store in an airtight container.

NUTRITIONAL INFORMATION: 320 calories | 8g protein | 30g carbs | 20g fat | 4g fiber | 0mg cholesterol | 10mg sodium | 300mg potassium.

QUICK TIP: Feel free to add or substitute with your favorite nuts or dried fruits!

NO-BAKE ENERGY BALLS

4 Serves | **10 min** Prep. | **0 min** Cook | Complexity ★★☆☆☆

INGREDIENTS
- 1 cup rolled oats
- 1/2 cup almond butter
- 1/3 cup honey
- 1/2 cup chocolate chips
- 1/4 cup chia seeds

DIRECTIONS
Mix all ingredients in a bowl. Shape into 1-inch balls. Chill for at least 20 minutes before serving.

NUTRITIONAL INFORMATION: 210 calories | 5g protein | 28g carbs | 10g fat | 5g fiber | 0mg cholesterol | 20mg sodium | 150mg potassium.

QUICK TIP: Add some protein powder for an extra boost!

Chapter 2: Bite-Size Snacks for Those Micro-Breaks

ROASTED CHICKPEAS

4 Serves | **5** min Prep. | **20** min Cook | Complexity ★★☆☆☆

INGREDIENTS
- 1 can (15 oz) of drained and rinsed chickpeas
- 1 tablespoon olive oil
- 1/2 teaspoon salt
- 1/4 teaspoon paprika

DIRECTIONS
Preheat oven to 400°F (200°C).
Toss chickpeas with olive oil, salt, and paprika.
Put chickpeas on a baking sheet and roast for 20 minutes, stirring them halfway through.

NUTRITIONAL INFORMATION: 150 calories | 6g protein | 20g carbs | 5g fat | 6g fiber | 0mg cholesterol | 400mg sodium | 180mg potassium.

QUICK TIP: Customize with your favorite spices! Try garlic powder, cayenne, or even cinnamon for a sweet twist!

SPEEDY VEGGIE CHIPS

4 Serves | **10** min Prep. | **5** min Cook | Complexity ★★☆☆☆

INGREDIENTS
- 2 zucchinis, thinly sliced
- 1 tablespoon olive oil
- Salt to taste

DIRECTIONS
Preheat your air fryer to 375°F (190°C).
Toss zucchini slices with olive oil and salt.
Air fry for 5 minutes or until crispy.

NUTRITIONAL INFORMATION: 70 calories | 1g protein | 6g carbs | 5g fat | 2g fiber | 0mg cholesterol | 50mg sodium | 300mg potassium.

QUICK TIP: No air fryer? No problem! You can bake these in the oven at 375°F (190°C) for 10-15 minutes.

FRUIT & NUT BARS

6 Serves | **10** min Prep. | **0** min Cook | Complexity ★★☆☆☆

INGREDIENTS
- 1 cup mixed nuts (almonds, cashews, walnuts)
- 1/2 cup dried fruit (cranberries, raisins)
- 1/4 cup honey

DIRECTIONS
Line a small tray or dish with parchment paper.
In a food processor, blend nuts and dried fruit until coarsely ground.
Stir in honey, then press the mixture into the tray. Chill for 20 minutes before cutting into bars.

NUTRITIONAL INFORMATION: 280 calories | 7g protein | 30g carbs | 16g fat | 4g fiber | 0mg cholesterol | 5mg sodium | 200mg potassium.

QUICK TIP: Add some dark chocolate chips for extra deliciousness!

QUICK RICE CAKE TOPPINGS

4 Serves | **5** min Prep. | **0** min Cook | Complexity ★☆☆☆☆

INGREDIENTS
- 4 rice cakes
- 1 avocado, mashed
- 1 tomato, sliced
- Salt and pepper to taste
- Optional: a sprinkle of red chili flakes

DIRECTIONS
Spread mashed avocado evenly on rice cakes.
Top with tomato slices.
Add salt, pepper, and a little chili flakes (optional).

NUTRITIONAL INFORMATION: 160 calories | 4g protein | 18g carbs | 9g fat | 4g fiber | 0mg cholesterol | 50mg sodium | 400mg potassium.

QUICK TIP: Experiment with other toppings like smoked salmon, cream cheese, or almond butter for variety.

Chapter 2: Bite-Size Snacks for Those Micro-Breaks 23

MINI VEGGIE WRAPS

| 4 Serves | 10 min Prep. | 0 min Cook | ★★☆☆☆ Complexity |

INGREDIENTS
- 4 lettuce leaves
- 1 carrot, julienned
- 1 cucumber, julienned
- 1 red bell pepper, julienned
- Optional: a drizzle of tahini or yogurt dressing

DIRECTIONS
Lay out the lettuce leaves flat on a plate.
Add julienned carrots, cucumber, and red bell pepper in the center.
Drizzle optional tahini or yogurt dressing.
Roll the lettuce leaves into wraps and enjoy.

NUTRITIONAL INFORMATION: 35 calories | 1g protein | 7g carbs | 0g fat | 2g fiber | 0mg cholesterol | 20mg sodium | 250mg potassium.

QUICK TIP: Add grilled chicken or tofu strips for extra protein.

OLIVE & CHEESE SKEWERS

| 4 Serves | 5 min Prep. | 0 min Cook | ★☆☆☆☆ Complexity |

INGREDIENTS
- 12 green olives
- 12 small cubes of feta cheese
- 4 toothpicks

DIRECTIONS
Thread 3 olives and 3 cheese cubes onto each toothpick.
Chill in the fridge for at least 10 minutes before serving.

NUTRITIONAL INFORMATION: 100 calories | 4g protein | 2g carbs | 8g fat | 1g fiber | 20mg cholesterol | 300mg sodium | 50mg potassium.

QUICK TIP: Add cherry tomatoes or small pieces of cucumber for extra flavor and color.

CUCUMBER & TUNA BITES

| 4 Serves | 10 min Prep. | 0 min Cook | Complexity ★★☆☆☆ |

INGREDIENTS
- 1 large cucumber, sliced
- 1 can (5 oz) tuna, drained
- 1 tablespoon mayonnaise
- Salt and pepper to taste
- Fresh dill for garnish

DIRECTIONS
Mix the tuna, mayonnaise, salt, and pepper in a bowl.
Spoon the tuna mixture onto cucumber slices.
Garnish with fresh dill.

NUTRITIONAL INFORMATION: 70 calories | 8g protein | 3g carbs | 3g fat | 1g fiber | 20mg cholesterol | 220mg sodium | 180mg potassium.

QUICK TIP: Use Greek yogurt instead of mayonnaise for a healthier option.

5-MINUTE SALSA & CHIPS

| 4 Serves | 5 min Prep. | 0 min Cook | Complexity ★☆☆☆☆ |

INGREDIENTS
- 1 can (14 oz) diced tomatoes, drained
- 1/2 onion, finely chopped
- 1 clove garlic, minced
- 1 jalapeño, finely chopped (optional)
- Salt and pepper to taste
- A bag of tortilla chips

DIRECTIONS
Mix tomatoes, onion, garlic, and optional jalapeño in a bowl.
Add salt and pepper to taste.
Serve immediately with tortilla chips.

NUTRITIONAL INFORMATION: 100 calories | 2g protein | 12g carbs | 5g fat | 2g fiber | 0mg cholesterol | 180mg sodium | 250mg potassium.

QUICK TIP: Leftover salsa? Use it as a topping for your morning eggs or lunchtime salads!

EASY VEGGIE SPRING ROLLS

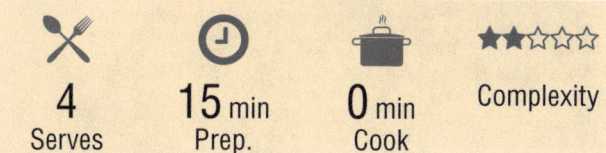

4 Serves | 15 min Prep. | 0 min Cook | Complexity ★★☆☆☆

INGREDIENTS
- Rice paper wrappers (8 pieces)
- 1 cup shredded carrots
- 1 cup thinly sliced cucumber
- 1 cup thinly sliced red bell pepper
- 1 avocado, sliced
- Fresh mint leaves (optional)
- Fresh cilantro leaves (optional)

DIRECTIONS
Briefly immerse the rice paper wrappers in warm water until they become pliable.
Spread a wrapper onto a flat surface and neatly place a portion of each vegetable in the middle.
Gently fold the sides of the wrapper over the veggies, then roll it up securely.
Continue this process with the rest of the wrappers and fillings.
(Optional) Serve alongside fresh mint or cilantro leaves for a refreshing touch.

NUTRITIONAL INFORMATION: 150 calories | 3g protein | 22g carbs | 6g fat | 5g fiber | 0mg cholesterol | 70mg sodium | 400mg potassium.

QUICK TIP: These are perfect for make-ahead snacks. Just wrap them in plastic wrap and refrigerate!

INSTANT SMOOTHIE POPS

6 Serves | 10 min Prep. | 2 hours freezing time | Complexity ★☆☆☆☆

INGREDIENTS
- 2 cups mixed frozen berries
- 1 banana, sliced
- 1 cup Greek yogurt
- 1 tablespoon honey

DIRECTIONS
Blend frozen berries, bananas, Greek yogurt, and honey until smooth.
Pour the mixture into popsicle molds.
Freeze for at least 2 hours or until firm.

NUTRITIONAL INFORMATION: 90 calories | 5g protein | 18g carbs | 1g fat | 3g fiber | 5mg cholesterol | 20mg sodium | 200mg potassium.

QUICK TIP: Don't have popsicle molds? Use an ice cube tray and toothpicks instead!

CHAPTER 3:
DIPS AND SIDES TO JAZZ UP YOUR MAIN COURSE

Chapter 3: Dips and Sides to Jazz Up Your Main Course

WHIPPED FETA

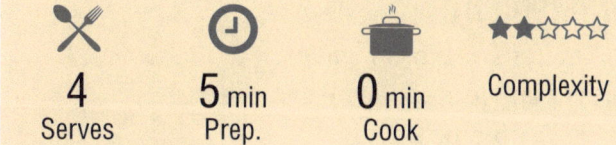

4 Serves | 5 min Prep. | 0 min Cook | Complexity ★★☆☆☆

INGREDIENTS
- 1 cup feta cheese
- 1/4 cup olive oil
- Juice of half a lemon
- 1 clove garlic, minced
- A pinch of salt and pepper

DIRECTIONS
Place feta, olive oil, lemon juice, and garlic in a blender.
Blend until smooth. Add salt and pepper to taste.

NUTRITIONAL INFORMATION: 190 calories | 6g protein | 2g carbs | 17g fat | 0g fiber | 25mg cholesterol | 320mg sodium | 50mg potassium.

QUICK TIP: This also makes a great sandwich spread!

5-MINUTE GUACAMOLE

4 Serves | 5 min Prep. | 0 min Cook | Complexity ★☆☆☆☆

INGREDIENTS
- 2 ripe avocados
- 1/2 onion, finely chopped
- Juice of 1 lime
- Salt and pepper to taste

DIRECTIONS
Mash the avocados in a bowl.
Add the onion and lime juice.
Season with salt and pepper.

NUTRITIONAL INFORMATION: 170 calories | 2g protein | 10g carbs | 15g fat | 7g fiber | 0mg cholesterol | 10mg sodium | 520mg potassium.

QUICK TIP: Got some brown avocado? Use it to make a face mask. Your skin will thank you!

GARLIC YOGURT SAUCE

6 Serves | 5 min Prep. | 0 min Cook | Complexity ★☆☆☆☆

INGREDIENTS
- 2 cups Greek yogurt
- 4 cloves garlic, minced
- 1 tablespoon olive oil
- Salt to taste

DIRECTIONS
Combine all ingredients in a bowl.
Mix well and serve.

NUTRITIONAL INFORMATION: 90 calories | 5g protein | 4g carbs | 6g fat | 0g fiber | 10mg cholesterol | 40mg sodium | 70mg potassium.

QUICK TIP: This sauce pairs well with grilled meats and veggies!

INSTANT PESTO

4 Serves | 5 min Prep. | 0 min Cook | Complexity ★★☆☆☆

INGREDIENTS
- 2 cups fresh basil leaves
- 1/2 cup grated Parmesan cheese
- 1/4 cup pine nuts
- 1/2 cup olive oil
- 2 cloves garlic
- Salt and pepper to taste

DIRECTIONS
Toss in basil, Parmesan, pine nuts, and garlic into the blender/food processor, or if you have more time and a mortar and pestle, grind them together to achieve a rough paste.
Pulse while gradually adding the olive oil.
Season with salt and pepper to taste.

NUTRITIONAL INFORMATION: 320 calories | 6g protein | 4g carbs | 30g fat | 1g fiber | 10mg cholesterol | 220mg sodium | 90mg potassium.

QUICK TIP: Running low on basil? Spinach makes a great substitute.

Chapter 3: Dips and Sides to Jazz Up Your Main Course   29

OLIVE TAPENADE

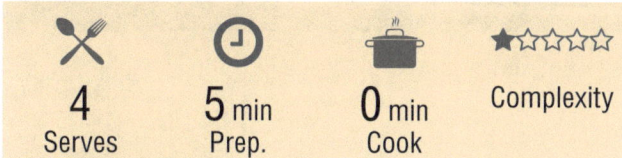

4 Serves | 5 min Prep. | 0 min Cook | Complexity

INGREDIENTS
- 1 cup pitted black olives
- 1 clove garlic
- 1 tablespoon capers
- 2 tablespoons olive oil
- Lemon zest to taste

DIRECTIONS
Add all ingredients to a food processor (or chop finely with a knife).
Pulse until smooth.
Season with lemon zest.

NUTRITIONAL INFORMATION: 100 calories | 1g protein | 2g carbs | 10g fat | 1g fiber | 0mg cholesterol | 500mg sodium | 40mg potassium.

QUICK TIP: This tapenade works wonders as a spread on a piece of crusty bread.

TOMATO & BASIL BRUSCHETTA

4 Serves | 5 min Prep. | 2 min Cook* | Complexity

*(toast the bread)

INGREDIENTS
- 4 slices of crusty bread
- 2 cups cherry tomatoes, halved
- 1/4 cup fresh basil, chopped
- 1 clove garlic, minced
- Olive oil for drizzling
- Salt and pepper to taste

DIRECTIONS
Toast the slices of bread.
In a bowl, mix cherry tomatoes, basil, and garlic.
Top each toast with the tomato mixture, drizzle with olive oil, and add salt and pepper.

NUTRITIONAL INFORMATION: 150 calories | 4g protein | 18g carbs | 7g fat | 2g fiber | 0mg cholesterol | 200mg sodium | 100mg potassium.

DID YOU KNOW? Basil isn't just for cooking; it's been used for centuries for its medicinal properties.

QUICK & ZESTY SALSA

4 Serves | 5 min Prep. | 0 min Cook | Complexity ★☆☆☆☆

INGREDIENTS
- 4 ripe tomatoes, diced
- 1 small onion, finely chopped
- 1 jalapeño, minced (seeds optional)
- Juice of 1 lime
- Handful of fresh cilantro, chopped
- Salt to taste

DIRECTIONS
In a bowl, combine all ingredients.
Mix well and let it sit for at least 10 minutes to allow flavors to blend.

NUTRITIONAL INFORMATION: 40 calories | 1g protein | 9g carbs | 0g fat | 2g fiber | 0mg cholesterol | 200mg sodium | 270mg potassium.

QUICK TIP: Great salsa is like a dance—spicy, lively, and best after a bit of practice.

SPEEDY VEGGIE STIR-FRY

2 Serves | 5 min Prep. | 7 min Cook | Complexity ★★☆☆☆

INGREDIENTS
- 2 cups mixed veggies (bell peppers, carrots, broccoli)
- 2 tablespoons soy sauce
- 1 tablespoon olive oil
- 1 clove garlic, minced

DIRECTIONS
Heat olive oil in a skillet.
Add veggies and garlic.
Stir-fry until tender.
Pour in soy sauce and cook for an additional minute.

NUTRITIONAL INFORMATION: 120 calories | 3g protein | 17g carbs | 5g fat | 4g fiber | 0mg cholesterol | 600mg sodium | 250mg potassium.

QUICK TIP: If you manage not to eat all the veggies during cooking, you're a stronger person than most of us.

Chapter 3: Dips and Sides to Jazz Up Your Main Course

FLASH-PICKLED VEGGIES

| 4 Serves | 5 min Prep. | 0 min Cook* | ★☆☆☆☆ Complexity |

* (let sit for at least 30 mins)

INGREDIENTS
- 2 cups sliced cucumber, carrot, or radish
- 1 cup vinegar
- 1 tablespoon sugar
- 1 teaspoon salt

DIRECTIONS
Place sliced veggies in a jar.

In a bowl, mix vinegar, sugar, and salt until dissolved.

Pour mixture over veggies and let sit for at least 30 minutes.

NUTRITIONAL INFORMATION: 20 calories | 0g protein | 4g carbs | 0g fat | 1g fiber | 0mg cholesterol | 600mg sodium | 70mg potassium.

QUICK TIP: Pickled veggies are the mullets of the culinary world: preparation business, party in flavor.

FRESH CORN SALAD

| 4 Serves | 10 min Prep. | 0 min Cook | ★★☆☆☆ Complexity |

INGREDIENTS
- 4 ears of corn, kernels removed
- 1 red bell pepper, diced
- 1/2 red onion, diced
- Juice of 1 lime
- Handful of fresh cilantro, chopped
- Salt and pepper to taste

DIRECTIONS
In a large bowl, combine all ingredients.
Toss well and serve immediately.

NUTRITIONAL INFORMATION: 90 calories | 3g protein | 20g carbs | 1g fat | 3g fiber | 0mg cholesterol | 10mg sodium | 270mg potassium.

DID YOU KNOW? Corn is a grain, a vegetable, and a fruit, making it the overachiever of the plant world.

ROASTED RED PEPPER DIP

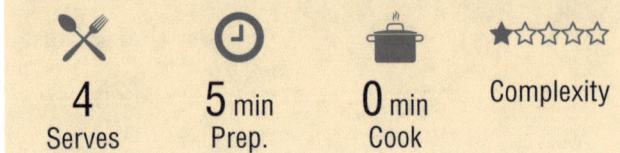

4 Serves | 5 min Prep. | 0 min Cook | Complexity

INGREDIENTS
- 1 jar (12 oz) of drained roasted red peppers
- 1 cup Greek yogurt or cream cheese
- 1 clove garlic, minced
- Salt and pepper to taste

DIRECTIONS
Blend roasted red peppers, Greek yogurt or cream cheese, and garlic in a food processor.
Add salt and pepper
Enjoy alongside your choice of chips or fresh veggies.

NUTRITIONAL INFORMATION: 90 calories | 6g protein | 6g carbs | 4g fat | 1g fiber | 5mg cholesterol | 260mg sodium | 180mg potassium.

QUICK TIP: Great as a pasta sauce, too! Talk about multitasking.

EASY QUINOA SALAD

4 Serves | 5 min Prep. | 20 min Cook* | Complexity

* (cook quinoa)

INGREDIENTS
- 2 cups cooked quinoa
- 1 cup diced cucumber
- 1 cup cherry tomatoes, halved
- 1/4 cup feta cheese, crumbled
- 1/4 cup olive oil
- Juice of 1 lemon
- Salt and pepper to taste

DIRECTIONS
In a large bowl, combine all ingredients.
Mix well and serve immediately or chill for later.

NUTRITIONAL INFORMATION: 220 calories | 5g protein | 24g carbs | 12g fat | 3g fiber | 5mg cholesterol | 240mg sodium | 350mg potassium.

QUICK TIP: If quinoa had a dating profile, it would be «health-conscious, versatile, and good with everything.»

Chapter 3: Dips and Sides to Jazz Up Your Main Course   33

FAST LEMON GARLIC ASPARAGUS

4 Serves | 5 min Prep. | 10 min Cook | Complexity

INGREDIENTS
- 1 bunch of asparagus, trimmed
- 2 tablespoons olive oil
- Juice of 1 lemon
- 2 cloves garlic, minced
- Salt and pepper to taste

DIRECTIONS
Preheat oven to 400°F (200°C).
Lay asparagus on a baking sheet
Drizzle with olive oil, lemon juice, and minced garlic.
Roast for 10 minutes or until tender.
Season with salt and pepper.

NUTRITIONAL INFORMATION: 70 calories | 3g protein | 6g carbs | 4g fat | 2g fiber | 0mg cholesterol | 150mg sodium | 220mg potassium.

QUICK TIP: Asparagus is an excellent source of vitamin K.

QUICK COLESLAW

4 Serves | 5 min Prep. | 0 min Cook | Complexity

INGREDIENTS
- 4 cups shredded cabbage
- 1 cup shredded carrots
- 1/2 cup mayonnaise
- 2 tablespoons vinegar
- Salt and pepper to taste

DIRECTIONS
In a bowl, mix all the ingredients until well combined.
Chill for 30 minutes before serving.

NUTRITIONAL INFORMATION: 180 calories | 1g protein | 8g carbs | 16g fat | 2g fiber | 10mg cholesterol | 300mg sodium | 140mg potassium.

QUICK TIP: Great for picnics and topping for pulled pork sandwiches! It's the extrovert of salads—good in any social situation.

CUCUMBER & MINT SALAD

| 4 Serves | 5 min Prep. | 0 min Cook | Complexity ★☆☆☆☆ |

INGREDIENTS
- 2 large cucumbers, sliced
- 1/4 cup fresh mint leaves, chopped
- Juice of 1 lemon
- Salt and pepper to taste

DIRECTIONS
In a large bowl, mix cucumbers, mint, and lemon juice.
Add salt and pepper to taste
Serve cold.

NUTRITIONAL INFORMATION: 20 calories | 1g protein | 5g carbs | 0g fat | 1g fiber | 0mg cholesterol | 5mg sodium | 150mg potassium.

DID YOU KNOW? Cucumbers are 95% water, making them the perfect snack for hydration or throwing in a water fight.

CHAPTER 4:
LIGHTNING-FAST LUNCHES FOR THE OFFICE OR HOME

TURKEY & AVOCADO WRAP

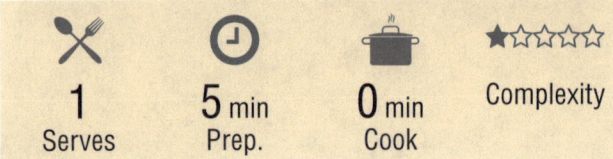

1 Serves | 5 min Prep. | 0 min Cook | Complexity ★☆☆☆☆

INGREDIENTS
- 1 whole-grain tortilla
- 4 slices turkey breast
- 1/2 avocado, sliced
- Lettuce leaves
- Salt and pepper to taste

DIRECTIONS
Lay the tortilla flat and layer turkey, avocado, and lettuce.
Add salt and pepper, roll it up, and it's ready to be enjoyed instantly!

NUTRITIONAL INFORMATION: 330 calories | 25g protein | 18g carbs | 18g fat | 7g fiber | 50mg cholesterol | 480mg sodium | 450mg potassium.

QUICK TIP: You can add some shredded cheese for extra flavor! It's like the party invite nobody turns down.

10-MINUTE CHICKEN CAESAR SALAD

2 Serves | 5 min Prep. | 5 min Cook* | Complexity ★★☆☆☆

* (cook chicken)

INGREDIENTS
- 2 cups romaine lettuce, torn
- 1 cup cooked chicken, sliced
- 1/4 cup Caesar dressing
- 1/4 cup croutons
- 2 tablespoons grated Parmesan cheese

DIRECTIONS
Combine lettuce, chicken, Caesar dressing, croutons, and Parmesan in a bowl.
Toss well and serve.

NUTRITIONAL INFORMATION: 280 calories | 20g protein | 12g carbs | 16g fat | 3g fiber | 50mg cholesterol | 420mg sodium | 230mg potassium.

QUICK TIP: No croutons? No worries! Crush up some crackers as a quick substitute. It's like the MacGyver of salads.

FLASH VEGGIE STIR-FRY

2 Serves | **5 min** Prep. | **5 min** Cook | ★★☆☆☆ Complexity

INGREDIENTS
- 2 cups mixed veggies (carrot, bell pepper, broccoli)
- 2 tablespoons soy sauce
- 1 tablespoon sesame oil
- 1 clove garlic, minced
- Salt and pepper to taste

DIRECTIONS
Heat oil in a pan and sauté garlic for a minute. Add mixed veggies and stir-fry until crispy but tender.
Add soy sauce and seasoning and stir to combine.

NUTRITIONAL INFORMATION: 110 calories | 3g protein | 12g carbs | 6g fat | 4g fiber | 0mg cholesterol | 560mg sodium | 300mg potassium.

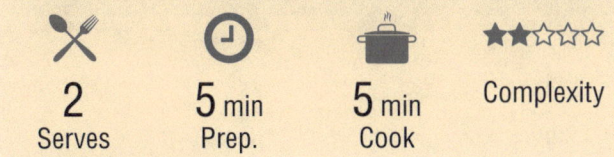

QUICK TIP: Running low on fresh veggies? Frozen vegetables work well, too! They're the understudies that never miss a cue.

CHICKPEA & SPINACH CURRY

4 Serves | **5 min** Prep. | **10 min** Cook | ★★☆☆☆ Complexity

INGREDIENTS
- 1 can (15 oz) chickpeas, drained
- 1 bag (10 oz) baby spinach
- 1 jar (12 oz) curry sauce
- Salt to taste

DIRECTIONS
Heat curry sauce in a pan, add chickpeas and spinach.
Cook until the spinach wilts and the chickpeas warm up. Add salt to taste.

NUTRITIONAL INFORMATION: 220 calories | 8g protein | 24g carbs | 10g fat | 6g fiber | 0mg cholesterol | 680mg sodium | 300mg potassium.

QUICK TIP: Want to feel like Popeye? Spinach is rich in iron, so go ahead and flex those muscles!

QUICK BBQ CHICKEN PIZZA

2 Serves | **5 min** Prep. | **10 min** Cook | Complexity ★★☆☆☆

INGREDIENTS
- 1 pre-made pizza crust
- 1/2 cup BBQ sauce
- 1 cup cooked chicken, shredded
- 1/2 cup shredded mozzarella
- 1/4 red onion, thinly sliced

DIRECTIONS
Spread BBQ sauce on the pizza crust.
Sprinkle with chicken, mozzarella, and red onion slices.
Cook in a 400°F oven for 10 minutes or until the cheese has melted.

NUTRITIONAL INFORMATION: 410 calories | 25g protein | 35g carbs | 18g fat | 2g fiber | 50mg cholesterol | 550mg sodium | 200mg potassium.

QUICK TIP: Craving Hawaiian? Toss on some pineapple chunks. Aloha, flavor!

SPICY TUNA SALAD

2 Serves | **5 min** Prep. | **0 min** Cook | Complexity ★☆☆☆☆

INGREDIENTS
- 1 can (5 oz) tuna, drained
- 1/4 cup mayo
- 1 tablespoon sriracha
- Salt and pepper to taste

DIRECTIONS
Mix tuna, mayo, sriracha, salt, and pepper in a bowl.
Serve on lettuce wraps or bread.

NUTRITIONAL INFORMATION: 210 calories | 13g protein | 2g carbs | 17g fat | 0g fiber | 40mg cholesterol | 310mg sodium | 110mg potassium.

QUICK TIP: Don't have sriracha? Any hot sauce will do! Spice is the variety of life.

Chapter 4: Lightning-Fast Lunches for the Office or Home

INSTANT RAMEN HACK

1 Serves | 3 min Prep. | 2 min Cook | Complexity: ★☆☆☆☆

INGREDIENTS
- 1 pack of instant ramen
- 1 cup water
- 1 egg
- Diced green onions for garnish

DIRECTIONS
Prepare the ramen noodles in hot water following the instructions on the package.

Crack an egg into the boiling water and cook to your liking.

Garnish with green onions.

NUTRITIONAL INFORMATION: 280 calories | 8g protein | 38g carbs | 10g fat | 2g fiber | 160mg cholesterol | 800mg sodium | 120mg potassium.

QUICK TIP: Toss frozen veggies to elevate your ramen game. It's like putting racing stripes on a sedan!

SPEEDY SPAGHETTI AGLIO E OLIO

2 Serves | 5 min Prep. | 10 min Cook | Complexity: ★★☆☆☆

INGREDIENTS
- 200g spaghetti
- 3 cloves garlic, sliced
- 1/4 cup olive oil
- Red pepper flakes to taste
- Salt and pepper to taste

DIRECTIONS
Cook the spaghetti according to the package instructions.

While the spaghetti is cooking, grab a separate pan, warm the olive oil, and gently sauté the garlic until it turns golden.

Stir in the red pepper flakes.

Once the spaghetti is done, drain it and toss it into the pan with the garlic and red pepper flakes. Give it a good mix to ensure all the flavors meld together. Add salt and pepper to taste, and it's ready to be served!

NUTRITIONAL INFORMATION: 420 calories | 10g protein | 50g carbs | 20g fat | 2g fiber | 0mg cholesterol | 10mg sodium | 120mg potassium.

QUICK TIP: No spaghetti? No problem! Linguini, fettuccine, or even ramen can fill in. It's the understudy that's always prepared!

VEGGIE & QUINOA BOWL

2 Serves | **5** min Prep. | **15** min Cook | Complexity ★★☆☆☆

INGREDIENTS
- 1 cup cooked quinoa
- 1 cup assorted veggies (e.g., bell peppers, zucchini)
- 1 tablespoon olive oil
- Salt and pepper to taste

DIRECTIONS
Sauté veggies in olive oil until tender.
Mix cooked quinoa and veggies in a bowl.
Season with salt and pepper.

NUTRITIONAL INFORMATION: 310 calories | 8g protein | 45g carbs | 12g fat | 5g fiber | 0mg cholesterol | 150mg sodium | 300mg potassium.

QUICK TIP: Meal prep hack! Separate a large batch into containers for a leisurely grab-and-go lunch!

15-MINUTE BEEF STIR-FRY

2 Serves | **5** min Prep. | **10** min Cook | Complexity ★★★☆☆

INGREDIENTS
- 1/2 lb beef strips
- 1 bell pepper, sliced
- 1 onion, sliced
- 2 tablespoons soy sauce
- 1 tablespoon olive oil

DIRECTIONS
Warm the oil in a skillet and sauté the beef until it turns brown.
Add bell pepper and onion, and sauté until softened.
Add soy sauce and stir well.

NUTRITIONAL INFORMATION: 280 calories | 25g protein | 10g carbs | 15g fat | 2g fiber | 50mg cholesterol | 800mg sodium | 320mg potassium.

QUICK TIP: No beef? Chicken or tofu can slide right in without missing a beat!

LENTIL & VEGGIE SALAD

2 Serves | **5 min** Prep. | **0 min** Cook | Complexity: ★☆☆☆☆

INGREDIENTS
- 1 cup cooked lentils
- 1/2 cucumber, diced
- 1 tomato, diced
- 1/4 cup feta cheese, crumbled
- 2 tablespoons olive oil
- Salt and pepper to taste

DIRECTIONS
In a bowl, combine lentils, cucumber, tomato, and feta.

Sprinkle olive oil, and add salt and pepper to taste.

NUTRITIONAL INFORMATION: 260 calories | 12g protein | 25g carbs | 14g fat | 6g fiber | 20mg cholesterol | 300mg sodium | 500mg potassium.

QUICK TIP: This salad is so versatile it should run for office. Add any veggies you like!

INSTANT POT CHICKEN RISOTTO

INGREDIENTS
- 1 cup Arborio rice
- 2 cups chicken broth
- 2 boneless, skinless chicken breasts
- 1/4 cup Parmesan cheese
- Salt and pepper to taste
- 1 tablespoon olive oil (optional)

DIRECTIONS

Cooking the Chicken using Instant Pot:

Add chicken breasts, a pinch of salt, and a cup of water or chicken broth to the Instant Pot.

Secure the lid and set the valve to sealing.

Press the «Poultry» button or set on Manual High Pressure for 10 minutes.

Once the cooking cycle is complete, allow for a Natural Pressure Release for 5 minutes, then do a Quick Release for any remaining pressure.

Remove chicken breasts and shred them using two forks.

Cooking the Chicken using Stovetop:

In a medium saucepan, bring water or chicken broth to a boil.

Add chicken breasts, reduce heat to low, cover, and simmer for 15-20 minutes, until chicken is cooked through.

Remove from heat, let it cool for a few minutes, then shred using two forks.

Making the Risotto:

Combine rice and 2 cups of chicken broth in the Instant Pot.

Cook on a manual for 7 minutes.

Once cooking is complete, do a Quick Release, then stir in the cooked, shredded chicken and Parmesan cheese, and season with salt and pepper to taste.

NUTRITIONAL INFORMATION: 350 calories | 20g protein | 40g carbs | 10g fat | 0g fiber | 40mg cholesterol | 800mg sodium | 200mg potassium.

QUICK TIP: This dish is perfect for a quick yet elegant dinner, and no one has to know it was made with the ease of an Instant Pot!

Serves: 4 | Prep: 10 min | Cook: 25 min | Complexity: ★★★☆☆

QUICK SHRIMP TACOS

INGREDIENTS
- 1/2 lb shrimp
- 2 tortillas
- 1/2 cup cabbage, shredded.
- 1/4 cup sour cream
- 1 tablespoon lime juice
- Salt and pepper to taste.

DIRECTIONS

Peeling and Deveining Shrimp

Lay the shrimp flat on a chopping board with the underside facing you.

Peel the shell off the legs and body in segments from the head end.

Use a small knife to make a shallow slit down the back of the shrimp.

Pull out the dark vein (or use the blade's tip) running along the back.

Cooking the Shrimp:

Heat a pan over medium-high heat.

Sauté shrimp in the pan until they turn pink and are cooked through, which should take 2-3 minutes on each side.

Assembling the Tacos:

Warm the tortillas in the oven or on the stovetop.

Mix the sour cream and lime juice in a small bowl.

Assemble tacos by layering shrimp, shredded cabbage, and a drizzle of sour cream mixture on each tortilla.

Season with salt and pepper to taste.

NUTRITIONAL INFORMATION: 280 calories | 22g protein | 20g carbs | 12g fat | 1g fiber | 160mg cholesterol | 500mg sodium | 200mg potassium.

QUICK TIP: Add a pinch of paprika to the shrimp while sautéing for an extra kick!

Serves: 2 | Prep: 10 min | Cook: 5 min | Complexity: ★★☆☆☆

FAST FALAFEL WRAP

2 Serves | **5 min** Prep. | **10 min** Cook | Complexity ★★☆☆☆

INGREDIENTS
- 4 pre-made falafel balls
- 2 tortillas
- 1/2 cup lettuce, shredded
- 1/4 cup hummus
- 1/2 tomato, diced

DIRECTIONS
Heat falafel according to package instructions.
Spread hummus on tortillas.
Add lettuce, falafel, and diced tomato.
Roll into a wrap.

NUTRITIONAL INFORMATION: 400 calories | 14g protein | 55g carbs | 12g fat | 7g fiber | 0mg cholesterol | 800mg sodium | 300mg potassium.

QUICK TIP: Hummus is the duct tape of the culinary world—it fixes everything. Add it for flavor, creaminess, and a protein boost!

EXPRESS CHICKEN QUESADILLA

1 Serves | **3 min** Prep. | **5 min** Cook | Complexity ★☆☆☆☆

INGREDIENTS
- 1 tortilla
- 1/2 cup cooked chicken, shredded
- 1/4 cup shredded cheese
- 1/4 cup salsa

DIRECTIONS
Place the tortilla in a non-stick pan.
Add chicken and cheese to half of the tortilla and fold.
Cook until the cheese turns melty and the tortilla gains a crispy edge, flipping once.
Serve with salsa on the side.

NUTRITIONAL INFORMATION: 350 calories | 20g protein | 25g carbs | 15g fat | 1g fiber | 50mg cholesterol | 600mg sodium | 150mg potassium.

QUICK TIP: Double or triple the ingredients if you cook for more people. Quesadillas are the «more the merrier» type!

CHAPTER 5:
SPEEDY DINNERS: SO YOU CAN GET ON WITH YOUR EVENING

ONE-POT MEDITERRANEAN CHICKEN

INGREDIENTS
- 4 boneless, skinless chicken breasts
- 1/4 cup olive oil
- 1 onion, chopped
- 3 garlic cloves, minced
- 1 cup cherry tomatoes, halved
- 1/2 cup black olives, pitted
- 1/4 cup feta cheese, crumbled
- 1 lemon, zested and juiced
- 2 tsp dried oregano
- Salt and pepper to taste

DIRECTIONS
Warm the olive oil over medium heat in a large skillet.
Lay the chicken breasts in the pan.
Add salt and pepper.
Allow them to cook until they brown on both sides.
Transfer the diced onion and minced garlic into the skillet, sautéing them until the onion is translucent.
Stir in the cherry tomatoes, black olives, lemon zest, lemon juice, and dried oregano.
Cover and simmer for 15 minutes or until the chicken is fully cooked.
Top with crumbled feta cheese before serving.

NUTRITIONAL INFORMATION: 320 calories | 28g protein | 9g carbs | 20g fat | 2g fiber | 85mg cholesterol | 450mg sodium | 500mg potassium.

QUICK TIP: This dish is best served with a side of quinoa or brown rice to soak up the delicious Mediterranean-flavored juices.

4 Serves | **15 min** Prep. | **25 min** Cook | Complexity ★★★☆☆

INSTANT POT CHILI

6 Serves | **10 min** Prep. | **20 min** Cook* | Complexity ★★☆☆☆

*(plus pressure building time)

INGREDIENTS
- 1 lb ground beef
- 1 onion, chopped
- 2 cloves garlic, minced
- 1 can (15 oz) diced tomatoes
- 1 can (15 oz) kidney beans, drained and rinsed
- 2 tbsp chili powder
- 1 tsp ground cumin
- 1/2 tsp paprika
- Salt and pepper to taste
- 1 cup beef broth

DIRECTIONS
Set your Instant Pot to «Sauté» mode and brown the ground beef.
Add the onions and garlic and continue to sauté until the onions are translucent.
Add the diced tomatoes, kidney beans, chili powder, cumin, paprika, salt, pepper, and beef broth. Stir well.
Close the lid and set the Instant Pot to «Manual» or «Pressure Cook» on high for 20 minutes.
Once done, release the pressure naturally for 10 minutes, then use the quick-release valve.

NUTRITIONAL INFORMATION: 265 calories | 20g protein | 20g carbs | 10g fat | 6g fiber | 55mg cholesterol | 410mg sodium | 650mg potassium.

QUICK TIP: Add shredded cheese, sour cream, and chopped green onions for flavor.

20-MINUTE BEEF & BROCCOLI

4 Serves | **10 min** Prep. | **10 min** Cook | Complexity ★★☆☆☆

INGREDIENTS
- 1 lb beef sirloin, thinly sliced
- 2 cups broccoli florets
- 3 tbsp soy sauce
- 2 cloves garlic, minced
- 1 tbsp ginger, grated
- 2 tbsp vegetable oil
- 2 tbsp oyster sauce
- 1 tsp cornstarch

DIRECTIONS
Heat the vegetable oil over medium-high heat in a large skillet or wok.
Add the beef and cook until browned.
Drop in the garlic and ginger, and sauté briefly for a minute.
Add the broccoli florets and stir-fry until tender but still crisp.
Mix the soy sauce, oyster sauce, and cornstarch in a bowl. Pour this mixture over the beef and broccoli and stir well.
Cook for another 2-3 minutes, until the sauce thickens slightly.

NUTRITIONAL INFORMATION: 295 calories | 25g protein | 9g carbs | 18g fat | 2g fiber | 70mg cholesterol | 860mg sodium | 500mg potassium.

QUICK TIP: Serve over steamed rice or noodles for a complete meal.

EASY BAKED SALMON

4 Serves | **5 min** Prep. | **15 min** Cook | Complexity ★★☆☆☆

INGREDIENTS
- 4 salmon fillets
- 2 tbsp olive oil
- 1 lemon, zested and juiced
- 2 cloves garlic, minced
- Salt and pepper to taste
- Fresh dill for garnish (optional)

DIRECTIONS
Preheat your oven to 375°F (190°C).
Place salmon fillets on a baking sheet lined with parchment paper.
Mix olive oil, lemon juice, lemon zest, salt, pepper, and minced garlic in a bowl.
Brush the mixture over each salmon fillet.
Bake in the oven for 12-15 minutes or until a fork can easily flake the salmon.
Garnish with fresh dill before serving, if desired.

NUTRITIONAL INFORMATION: 240 calories | 23g protein | 0g carbs | 15g fat | 0g fiber | 65mg cholesterol | 70mg sodium | 400mg potassium.

QUICK TIP: Pair this salmon with steamed asparagus or roasted vegetables for a wholesome meal.

FAST VEGETABLE CURRY

4 Serves | **5 min** Prep. | **15 min** Cook | Complexity ★★☆☆☆

INGREDIENTS
- 2 cups mixed vegetables (broccoli, bell peppers, carrots)
- 1 can (14 oz) coconut milk
- 3 tablespoons curry paste
- Salt to taste

DIRECTIONS
Sauté mixed vegetables in a large pan until slightly softened.
Add curry paste and coconut milk.
Simmer for 10 minutes.
Season with salt.

NUTRITIONAL INFORMATION: 80 calories | 3g protein | 15g carbs | 20g fat | 4g fiber | 0mg cholesterol | 500mg sodium | 300mg potassium.

QUICK TIP: Leftovers are great for lunch the next day—assuming you can resist eating it all tonight!

LEMON GARLIC SHRIMP PASTA

4 Serves | **10** min Prep. | **15** min Cook | ★★★☆☆ Complexity

INGREDIENTS
- 8 oz linguine or spaghetti
- 1 lb large shrimp, peeled and deveined
- 4 cloves garlic, minced
- 1 lemon, zested and juiced
- 1/4 cup white wine (or you can use chicken broth)
- 2 tbsp olive oil
- 1/4 cup fresh parsley, chopped
- Salt and pepper to taste
- A dash of red pepper flakes (only if you like a little heat!)

Peeling and Deveining Shrimp
Lay the shrimp flat on a chopping board with the underside facing you.
Peel the shell off the legs and body in segments from the head end.
Use a small knife to make a shallow slit down the back of the shrimp.
Gently pull out the dark vein (or use the blade's tip) running along the back.
Rinse the shrimp under cold water if necessary.

DIRECTIONS
Begin by preparing the shrimp as per the steps above if they are not already peeled and deveined.
Cook the pasta according to the package instructions until al dente. Once cooked, drain well and set aside.
In a large skillet, warm the olive oil over medium heat. Add the garlic and sauté for about a minute or until it becomes fragrant.
Add the prepared shrimp to the skillet and cook until they turn pink on both sides, which should take about 2-3 minutes per side.
Pour in the white wine (or chicken broth) and the lemon juice, stirring well to lift any tasty bits from the bottom of the skillet.
Add the cooked pasta to the shrimp mixture in the skillet. Toss everything well to combine, and season with salt, pepper, and a dash of red pepper flakes if desired.
Garnish with fresh parsley and a sprinkle of lemon zest, give it one last good toss, and serve immediately!

NUTRITIONAL INFORMATION: 400 calories | 28g protein | 45g carbs | 10g fat | 2g fiber | 180mg cholesterol | 310mg sodium | 250mg potassium.

QUICK TIP: For a creamier version, feel free to add a splash of heavy cream or a dollop of cream cheese while wrapping up the cooking process.

QUICK CHICKEN ALFREDO

| 2 Serves | 5 min Prep. | 10 min Cook | Complexity ★★☆☆☆ |

INGREDIENTS
- 2 cups cooked fettuccine
- 1 cup cooked chicken, shredded
- 1/2 cup Alfredo sauce
- Grated Parmesan cheese for garnish

DIRECTIONS
Heat Alfredo sauce in a pan.
Add cooked chicken and pasta, stirring until heated through.
Garnish with Parmesan cheese.

NUTRITIONAL INFORMATION: 580 calories | 30g protein | 50g carbs | 25g fat | 2g fiber | 90mg cholesterol | 700mg sodium | 250mg potassium.

QUICK TIP: No time for dessert? Grate extra cheese — it's the Parmesan sprinkle on the cake of life.

SPEEDY SHEET PAN FAJITAS

| 4 Serves | 5 min Prep. | 20 min Cook | Complexity ★☆☆☆☆ |

INGREDIENTS
- 2 bell peppers, sliced
- 1 onion, sliced
- 1 lb chicken breast, sliced
- 1 packet fajita seasoning

DIRECTIONS
Preheat oven to 400°F (200°C).
Toss all ingredients with fajita seasoning.
Lay out evenly on a baking sheet and let bake for 20 minutes.

NUTRITIONAL INFORMATION: 270 calories | 25g protein | 10g carbs | 15g fat | 2g fiber | 70mg cholesterol | 600mg sodium | 220mg potassium.

QUICK TIP: For a vegetarian twist, swap chicken with portobello mushrooms.

Dinner doesn't have to be a three-hour cooking marathon. With these speedy recipes, you can enjoy a delicious meal and still have time for the things you love. Enjoy!

Chapter 5: Speedy Dinners So You Can Get On With Your Evening

INSTANT POT PULLED PORK

6 Serves | **5 min** Prep. | **45 min** Cook* | ★★★☆☆ Complexity

* (Instant Pot magic!)

INGREDIENTS
- 2 lbs pork shoulder
- 1 cup BBQ sauce
- 1/2 cup water

DIRECTIONS
Place pork shoulder, BBQ sauce, and water in the Instant Pot.
Set to Pressure Cook on High for 45 minutes.
Use natural release, then shred the meat with forks.

NUTRITIONAL INFORMATION: 350 calories | 22g protein | 25g carbs | 15g fat | 1g fiber | 70mg cholesterol | 550mg sodium | 300mg potassium.

QUICK TIP: Slap it on a bun for a pulled pork sandwich or wrap it in a tortilla with some slaw. This pork is a social chameleon.

15-MINUTE FISH TACOS

4 Serves | **5 min** Prep. | **10 min** Cook | ★☆☆☆☆ Complexity

INGREDIENTS
- 1 lb white fish fillets
- 8 small corn tortillas
- 1/2 cabbage, shredded
- 1 lime, cut into wedges

DIRECTIONS
Cook fish fillets in a pan until flaky.
Warm tortillas.
Assemble tacos with fish and shredded cabbage and serve with lime wedges.

NUTRITIONAL INFORMATION: 210 calories | 20g protein | 20g carbs | 6g fat | 3g fiber | 40mg cholesterol | 200mg sodium | 200mg potassium.

QUICK TIP: To taco or not to taco? That's a silly question.

QUICK CAULIFLOWER FRIED RICE

4 Serves | **5** min Prep. | **10** min Cook | Complexity ★★☆☆☆

INGREDIENTS
- 4 cups cauliflower rice
- 2 eggs, scrambled
- 1 cup frozen peas and carrots
- 3 tablespoons soy sauce

DIRECTIONS
Sauté cauliflower rice in a pan until tender.
Add scrambled eggs, peas, and carrots, and mix well.
Blend in the soy sauce and keep it on the heat for 2 more minutes.

NUTRITIONAL INFORMATION: 150 calories | 10g protein | 15g carbs | 5g fat | 5g fiber | 90mg cholesterol | 500mg sodium | 300mg potassium.

QUICK TIP: Cauliflower is the spy of the veggie world, seamlessly blending into dishes like rice and pizza crust.

EASY LEMON HERB CHICKEN

4 Serves | **5** min Prep. | **20** min Cook | Complexity ★★☆☆☆

INGREDIENTS
- 4 boneless chicken breasts
- 1 lemon, sliced
- Fresh herbs (thyme, rosemary)
- Salt and pepper to taste

DIRECTIONS
Place chicken breasts in a baking dish.
Top with lemon slices and fresh herbs.
Bake at 375°F (190°C) for 20 minutes or until chicken is cooked through.

NUTRITIONAL INFORMATION: 220 calories | 28g protein | 2g carbs | 9g fat | 0g fiber | 80mg cholesterol | 220mg sodium | 250mg potassium.

QUICK TIP: When life gives you lemons, make lemon herb chicken. It's better than lemonade.

Chapter 5: Speedy Dinners So You Can Get On With Your Evening 53

EXPRESS BEEF STROGANOFF

4 Serves | **5 min** Prep. | **15 min** Cook | Complexity ★★☆☆☆

INGREDIENTS
- 1 lb beef strips
- 1 cup mushroom slices
- 1 onion, chopped
- 1 cup sour cream
- Salt and pepper to taste

DIRECTIONS
Sauté beef strips and onions until browned.
Throw in mushrooms and continue cooking for another 3 minutes.
Stir in sour cream and season with salt and pepper.
Serve hot over noodles or rice.

NUTRITIONAL INFORMATION: 400 calories | 22g protein | 12g carbs | 25g fat | 2g fiber | 90mg cholesterol | 400mg sodium | 200mg potassium.

QUICK TIP: Serve it over egg noodles to make friends across borders.

SPEEDY SWEET & SOUR CHICKEN

4 Serves | **5 min** Prep. | **15 min** Cook | Complexity ★☆☆☆☆

INGREDIENTS
- 1 lb chicken pieces
- 1 can (14 oz) pineapple chunks, drained
- 1/4 cup ketchup
- 1/4 cup vinegar
- 2 tbsp sugar

DIRECTIONS
Cook chicken pieces in a skillet until no longer pink.
In a separate bowl, mix pineapple, ketchup, vinegar, and sugar.
Pour sauce over chicken and simmer for 10 minutes.

NUTRITIONAL INFORMATION: 280 calories | 24g protein | 25g carbs | 8g fat | 1g fiber | 80mg cholesterol | 300mg sodium | 200mg potassium.

QUICK TIP: Forget takeout; this is a fast-food hack you can feel good about!

QUICK GREEK GYROS

4 Serves | **5** min Prep. | **10** min Cook | Complexity

INGREDIENTS
- 1 lb gyro meat or sliced lamb/beef/chicken
- 4 pieces of pita bread
- 1 cup tzatziki sauce
- 1 tomato, diced
- 1 onion, sliced

DIRECTIONS
In a skillet, cook the meat until it achieves a browned color.
Warm the pita bread.
Assemble gyros with meat, tzatziki sauce, diced tomato, and sliced onion.

NUTRITIONAL INFORMATION: 320 calories | 24g protein | 25g carbs | 12g fat | 2g fiber | 70mg cholesterol | 600mg sodium | 200mg potassium.

QUICK TIP: Just like a vacation in Mykonos but without the travel time!

CHAPTER 6:
5-INGREDIENT WONDERS

5-INGREDIENT BLACK BEAN SOUP

4 Serves | **5** min Prep. | **20** min Cook | Complexity

INGREDIENTS
- 2 cans of rinsed and drained black beans
- 4 cups chicken or vegetable broth
- 1 onion, chopped
- 2 cloves garlic, minced
- Salt to taste

DIRECTIONS
In a pot, sauté onion and garlic until translucent. Add in the beans and broth, then heat the mixture to a boil.
Use a hand blender to puree until smooth.
Season with salt and serve hot.

NUTRITIONAL INFORMATION: 190 calories | 10g protein | 25g carbs | 3g fat | 10g fiber | 0mg cholesterol | 500mg sodium | 300mg potassium.

QUICK TIP: Less is more—sometimes just 5 ingredients can warm your soul.

5-INGREDIENT MARGHERITA PIZZA

2 Serves | **5** min Prep. | **10** min Cook | Complexity

INGREDIENTS
- 1 ready-made pizza crust
- 1 cup tomato sauce
- 1 cup shredded mozzarella
- 1/2 cup fresh basil leaves
- 1 tbsp olive oil

DIRECTIONS
Preheat oven as per pizza crust instructions. Spread tomato sauce and mozzarella on the crust. Bake until the cheese is melted and the crust turns a golden hue.
Top with fresh basil and a drizzle of olive oil before serving.

NUTRITIONAL INFORMATION: 390 calories | 15g protein | 45g carbs, 15g fat | 3g fiber | 20mg cholesterol | 800mg sodium | 250mg potassium.

QUICK TIP: When you need pizza pronto, 5 ingredients will get you there!

Chapter 6: 5-Ingredient Wonders

5-INGREDIENT CHICKEN STIR-FRY

4 Serves | **5** min Prep. | **15-20** min Cook | Complexity ★☆☆☆☆

INGREDIENTS
- 1 lb chicken strips
- 4 cups mixed vegetables
- 1/4 cup soy sauce
- 2 tbsp oil
- Salt and pepper to taste

DIRECTIONS
Heat oil in a pan over medium-high heat. Once the oil is hot, add the chicken strips.
Cook the chicken strips for about 5-7 minutes until they're no longer pink in the center, and have a minimum internal temperature of 165°F (74°C). It's helpful to use a meat thermometer to ensure the chicken is cooked safely.
Add the mixed vegetables to the pan with the chicken, and stir-fry for 7-10 minutes, or until the vegetables are tender yet crisp.
Stir in the soy sauce, and season with salt and pepper to taste. Toss everything together well before serving.

NUTRITIONAL INFORMATION: 240 calories | 20g protein | 20g carbs | 8g fat | 5g fiber | 40mg cholesterol | 600mg sodium | 300mg potassium.

QUICK TIP: Stir-fries are the epitome of fast food—fast to cook, fast to eat, and fast to clean up! Plus, they are incredibly versatile; feel free to switch up the vegetables or protein to match what you have on hand.

5-INGREDIENT PASTA CARBONARA

4 Serves | **5** min Prep. | **12** min Cook | Complexity ★★☆☆☆

INGREDIENTS
- 8 oz spaghetti
- 4 oz pancetta or bacon, diced
- 2 eggs
- 1 cup grated Parmesan
- Salt and pepper to taste

DIRECTIONS
Cook spaghetti according to package instructions.
Using another pan, crisp up the pancetta by frying it.
Beat eggs with Parmesan, salt, and pepper.
Mix everything, using pasta water to thin sauce if needed.

NUTRITIONAL INFORMATION: 420 calories | 18g protein | 40g carbs | 20g fat | 2g fiber | 100mg cholesterol | 800mg sodium | 150mg potassium.

QUICK TIP: Skip the Italian restaurant; you're 5 ingredients away from *la dolce vita* at home!

5-INGREDIENT VEGGIE TACOS

4 Serves | **5** min Prep. | **10** min Cook | Complexity

INGREDIENTS
- 8 small corn tortillas
- 2 cups of drained and rinsed canned black beans
- 1 avocado, sliced
- 1 cup salsa
- 1 lime, cut into wedges

DIRECTIONS
Heat the black beans on the stove.
Warm the tortillas in a skillet.
Assemble tacos with black beans, avocado slices, and salsa.
Serve with lime wedges.

NUTRITIONAL INFORMATION: 220 calories | 8g protein | 40g carbs | 6g fat | 10g fiber | 0mg cholesterol | 400mg sodium | 500mg potassium.

QUICK TIP: Tacos aren't just for Tuesdays; they're for any day you have 5 ingredients and 15 minutes!

5-INGREDIENT BEEF & RICE

4 Serves | **5** min Prep. | **20** min Cook | Complexity

INGREDIENTS
- 1 lb ground beef
- 2 cups cooked rice
- 1 cup beef broth
- 1 onion, chopped
- Salt and pepper to taste

DIRECTIONS
In a skillet, brown the ground beef and onion.
Stir in cooked rice and beef broth.
Simmer until the mixture thickens.
Season with salt and pepper.

NUTRITIONAL INFORMATION: 380 calories | 25g protein | 45g carbs | 12g fat | 2g fiber | 70mg cholesterol | 300mg sodium | 250mg potassium.

QUICK TIP: Save even more time by using leftover rice from last night's dinner.

Chapter 6: 5-Ingredient Wonders   59

5-INGREDIENT FISH & CHIPS

4 Serves | **5** min Prep. | **20** min Cook | Complexity ★★☆☆☆

INGREDIENTS
- 4 fish fillets
- 4 large potatoes, sliced
- 1 cup flour
- Salt and cooking oil
- Lemon wedges for serving

DIRECTIONS
Heat the oil using a deep fryer or a big pan.
Dredge fish fillets in flour, seasoned with salt.
Fry fish and potato slices until golden.
Serve with lemon wedges.

NUTRITIONAL INFORMATION: 550 calories | 35g protein | 65g carbs | 15g fat | 3g fiber | 85mg cholesterol | 500mg sodium | 1100mg potassium.

QUICK TIP: Sometimes, the simplest things bring the most joy, like this classic comfort food.

5-INGREDIENT EGG FRIED RICE

4 Serves | **5** min Prep. | **10** min Cook | Complexity ★☆☆☆☆

INGREDIENTS
- 3 cups cooked rice
- 4 eggs, beaten
- 1/4 cup soy sauce
- 2 green onions, chopped
- 1 tbsp oil

DIRECTIONS
Heat oil in a wok or skillet.
Add beaten eggs and scramble until cooked.
Stir in rice and soy sauce.
Garnish with green onions before serving.

NUTRITIONAL INFORMATION: 280 calories | 10g protein | 45g carbs | 5g fat | 1g fiber | 180mg cholesterol | 800mg sodium | 150mg potassium.

QUICK TIP: Make it a breakfast-for-dinner night with this versatile dish!

5-INGREDIENT TOMATO BASIL SOUP

4 Serves | **5 min** Prep. | **20 min** Cook | Complexity ★☆☆☆☆

INGREDIENTS
- 1 can (28 oz) crushed tomatoes
- 2 cups chicken or vegetable broth
- 1/2 cup fresh basil leaves
- 1 cup cream
- Salt and pepper to taste

DIRECTIONS
In a pot, combine tomatoes and broth. Bring to a simmer.
Add basil leaves into the mix and blend in the blender to a smooth consistency.
Stir in cream and season with salt and pepper.

NUTRITIONAL INFORMATION: 240 calories | 4g protein | 20g carbs | 15g fat | 3g fiber | 50mg cholesterol | 500mg sodium | 250mg potassium.

QUICK TIP: For a vegan version, swap out the cream for coconut milk.

5-INGREDIENT PANCAKES

4 Serves | **5 min** Prep. | **10 min** Cook | Complexity ★☆☆☆☆

INGREDIENTS
- 1 cup flour
- 1 cup milk
- 1 egg
- 1 tbsp sugar
- 1 tbsp baking powder

DIRECTIONS
In a bowl, mix all the ingredients until smooth.
Heat a skillet and drop in spoonfuls of batter.
Flip when bubbles form on the surface.
Serve hot with your favorite toppings.

NUTRITIONAL INFORMATION: 210 calories | 6g protein | 40g carbs | 3g fat | 1g fiber | 50mg cholesterol | 300mg sodium | 150mg potassium.

QUICK TIP: Save time in the morning by mixing the dry ingredients the night before.

CHAPTER 7:
SATISFY THAT SWEET TOOTH IN MINUTES

3-INGREDIENT COOKIES

12 Cookies | **5 min** Prep. | **12 min** Cook | Complexity ★☆☆☆☆

INGREDIENTS
- 2 ripe bananas, mashed
- 1 cup oats
- 1/2 cup chocolate chips

DIRECTIONS
Preheat oven to 350°F (175°C).
Mix all ingredients in a bowl.
Drop spoonfuls onto a baking sheet.
Bake for 12 minutes.

NUTRITIONAL INFORMATION: 100 calories | 2g protein | 18g carbs | 3g fat | 2g fiber | 0mg cholesterol | 10mg sodium | 80mg potassium.

QUICK TIP: Not a chocolate fan? Swap out the chips for dried fruit!

QUICK BERRY SORBET

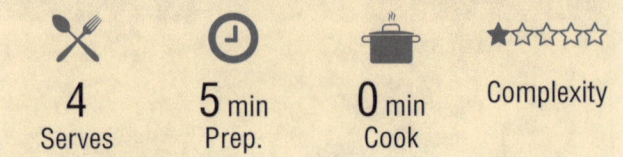

4 Serves | **5 min** Prep. | **0 min** Cook | Complexity ★☆☆☆☆

INGREDIENTS
- 4 cups frozen berries
- 1/4 cup sugar
- 1/4 cup water

DIRECTIONS
Blend all ingredients until smooth.
Serve immediately or store in the freezer.

NUTRITIONAL INFORMATION: 100 calories | 1g protein | 25g carbs | 0g fat | 3g fiber | 0mg cholesterol | 0mg sodium | 100mg potassium.

QUICK TIP: It tastes like summer, even when it's snowing outside.

Chapter 7: Satisfy That Sweet Tooth in Minutes

INSTANT CHOCO-MOUSSE

4 Serves | **5** min Prep. | **0** min Cook | Complexity ★☆☆☆☆

INGREDIENTS
- 1 can (14 oz) coconut milk
- 1/4 cup cocoa powder
- 1/4 cup sugar

DIRECTIONS
Mix all ingredients in a blender until smooth. Place in the fridge to chill for at least 1 hour.

NUTRITIONAL INFORMATION: 200 calories | 2g protein | 15g carbs | 16g fat | 2g fiber | 0mg cholesterol | 30mg sodium | 180mg potassium.

QUICK TIP: Use a frozen banana for a fruity twist!

SPEEDY FRUIT SALAD

4 Serves | **5** min Prep. | **0** min Cook | Complexity ★☆☆☆☆

INGREDIENTS
- 4 cups mixed fruit (your choice)
- 1 cup yogurt
- 1/4 cup honey

DIRECTIONS
Mix all ingredients in a large bowl. Serve chilled.

NUTRITIONAL INFORMATION: 150 calories | 3g protein | 35g carbs | 0g fat | 2g fiber | 0mg cholesterol | 30mg sodium | 150mg potassium.

QUICK TIP: Serve this on top of pancakes for a fruitful breakfast.

NO-BAKE CHEESECAKE CUPS

4 Serves | **10** min Prep. | **0** min Cook | Complexity ★★☆☆☆

INGREDIENTS
- 8 oz cream cheese, softened
- 1 cup graham cracker crumbs
- 1/2 cup sugar
- 1/2 cup heavy cream
- 1 tsp vanilla extract

DIRECTIONS
Blend cream cheese, sugar, and vanilla in a bowl until smooth.
Whip the heavy cream until stiff peaks form.
Lightly fold the whipped cream into the creamy cheese blend.
Layer graham cracker crumbs and cream cheese mixture in cups.
Chill for at least 1 hour.

NUTRITIONAL INFORMATION: 450 calories | 6g protein | 40g carbs | 30g fat | 1g fiber | 100mg cholesterol | 200mg sodium | 100mg potassium.

QUICK TIP: Add a dollop of your favorite fruit jam on top for extra flavor!

5-MINUTE BROWNIES

9 Serves | **3** min Prep. | **2** min Cook* | Complexity ★☆☆☆☆

* (microwave)

INGREDIENTS
- 1/2 cup melted butter
- 1 cup sugar
- 2 eggs
- 1/2 cup cocoa powder
- 1/2 cup flour

DIRECTIONS
In a bowl, mix all ingredients.
Pour into a microwave-safe dish.
Microwave for 2 minutes on high.

NUTRITIONAL INFORMATION: 250 calories | 4g protein | 35g carbs | 12g fat | 2g fiber | 50mg cholesterol | 120mg sodium | 90mg potassium.

QUICK TIP: Throw in some chocolate chips or nuts for an extra twist!

Chapter 7: Satisfy That Sweet Tooth in Minutes

QUICK APPLE CRISP

4 Serves | **5 min** Prep. | **20 min** Cook | Complexity ★★☆☆☆

INGREDIENTS
- 4 apples, sliced
- 1/2 cup oats
- 1/4 cup sugar
- 1/4 cup butter
- 1/2 tsp cinnamon

DIRECTIONS
Preheat oven to 350°F (175°C).
Place apple slices in a baking dish.
Mix oats, sugar, butter, and cinnamon.
Sprinkle mixture over apples.
Bake for 20 minutes.

NUTRITIONAL INFORMATION: 200 calories | 2g protein | 35g carbs | 8g fat | 4g fiber | 30mg cholesterol | 100mg sodium | 130mg potassium.

QUICK TIP: Enjoy it warm, topped with a scoop of vanilla ice cream!

FAST & EASY LEMON BARS

9 Bars | **10 min** Prep. | **15 min** Cook | Complexity ★★☆☆☆

INGREDIENTS
- 1 cup flour
- 1/2 cup butter, melted
- 1/2 cup sugar
- 2 lemons, juiced
- 2 eggs

DIRECTIONS
Preheat oven to 350°F (175°C).
Mix flour, butter, and half the sugar, and press into a pan.
Mix lemon juice, remaining sugar, and eggs.
Pour over the crust.
Bake for 15 minutes.

NUTRITIONAL INFORMATION: 220 calories | 3g protein | 30g carbs | 11g fat | 1g fiber | 60mg cholesterol | 90mg sodium | 50mg potassium.

QUICK TIP: Great as a tangy treat for summer picnics!

INSTANT FROZEN YOGURT

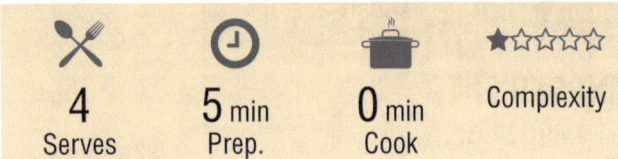

4 Serves | **5** min Prep. | **0** min Cook | Complexity ★☆☆☆☆

INGREDIENTS
- 4 cups frozen fruit (your choice)
- 1 cup yogurt
- 1/4 cup honey

DIRECTIONS
Blend all ingredients until smooth.
Serve immediately or store in the freezer.

NUTRITIONAL INFORMATION: 130 calories | 3g protein | 30g carbs | 1g fat | 2g fiber | 5mg cholesterol | 40mg sodium | 100mg potassium.

QUICK TIP: This also works great as a smoothie!

10-MINUTE RICE PUDDING

4 Serves | **3** min Prep. | **7** min Cook | Complexity ★☆☆☆☆

INGREDIENTS
- 2 cups cooked rice
- 1 cup milk
- 1/2 cup sugar
- 1 tsp vanilla
- 1/2 tsp cinnamon

DIRECTIONS
Mix all ingredients in a pot.
Maintain a medium heat and stir continuously for 7 minutes.

NUTRITIONAL INFORMATION: 220 calories | 4g protein | 45g carbs | 2g fat | 0g fiber | 5mg cholesterol | 40mg sodium | 100mg potassium.

QUICK TIP: Add raisins or nuts for added texture!

Chapter 7: Satisfy That Sweet Tooth in Minutes

NO-BAKE OAT COOKIES

12 Cookies | **5** min Prep. | **0** min Cook | Complexity

INGREDIENTS
- 1 cup oats
- 1/2 cup peanut butter
- 1/4 cup honey
- 1/2 cup chocolate chips
- 1/2 teaspoon vanilla extract

DIRECTIONS
In a bowl, mix all ingredients.
Form into small balls and flatten on a parchment-lined tray.
Chill in the fridge for at least 30 minutes.

NUTRITIONAL INFORMATION: 150 calories | 4g protein | 20g carbs | 7g fat | 2g fiber | 0mg cholesterol | 60mg sodium | 90mg potassium.

QUICK TIP: No oven? No problem! These cookies are a no-bake miracle.

QUICKIE CHOCOLATE FONDUE

4 Serves | **2** min Prep. | **3** min Cook | Complexity

INGREDIENTS
- 1 cup chocolate chips
- 1/2 cup heavy cream
- Assorted fruits for dipping

DIRECTIONS
In a microwave-safe bowl, melt the chocolate chips and cream together.
Stir until smooth.
Serve with fruits for dipping.

NUTRITIONAL INFORMATION: 300 calories | 2g protein | 35g carbs | 20g fat | 2g fiber | 30mg cholesterol | 20mg sodium | 90mg potassium.

QUICK TIP: Fondue isn't just for fancy dinners; it's an express lane to the Chocolate Nirvana Highway.

SPEEDY TIRAMISU CUPS

4 Serves | **10** min Prep. | **0** min Cook | ★★★☆☆ Complexity

INGREDIENTS
- 1 cup mascarpone cheese
- 1/2 cup heavy cream
- 1/4 cup sugar
- 1 cup brewed coffee, cooled
- 8 ladyfingers
- Cocoa powder for dusting

DIRECTIONS
Whip the mascarpone, heavy cream, and sugar until smooth.
Dip ladyfingers in coffee and layer in cups.
Alternate with cheese mixture.
Dust with cocoa powder and chill for at least 30 minutes.

NUTRITIONAL INFORMATION: 380 calories | 5g protein | 30g carbs | 25g fat | 1g fiber | 80mg cholesterol | 100mg sodium | 80mg potassium.

QUICK TIP: Tiramisu translates to «pick me up,» and with this speed, it's also a «put me down» because you'll finish it so fast!

EASY BANANA BREAD MUG CAKE

1 Serves | **3** min Prep. | **2** min Cook* | ★☆☆☆☆ Complexity

* (microwave)

INGREDIENTS
- 1 ripe banana
- 4 tablespoons flour
- 2 tablespoons sugar
- 1/4 teaspoon baking powder
- 1 tablespoon melted butter

DIRECTIONS
Mash the banana in a microwave-safe mug.
Add remaining ingredients and mix.
Microwave for 2 minutes.

NUTRITIONAL INFORMATION: 300 calories | 3g protein | 60g carbs | 7g fat | 3g fiber | 15mg cholesterol | 60mg sodium | 400mg potassium.

QUICK TIP: Feel like a baker without the bake time!

Chapter 7: Satisfy That Sweet Tooth in Minutes 69

INSTANT S'MORES

4 Serves | **2** min Prep. | **1** min Cook* | Complexity

*(microwave)

INGREDIENTS
- 8 graham crackers
- 4 marshmallows
- 4 pieces of chocolate

DIRECTIONS
Assemble the graham cracker, marshmallow, and chocolate.

Microwave for 10–20 seconds until marshmallow puffs up.

Top with another graham cracker.

NUTRITIONAL INFORMATION: 150 calories | 2g protein | 25g carbs | 6g fat | 1g fiber | 5mg cholesterol | 100mg sodium | 50mg potassium.

QUICK TIP: Instant S'mores: When you want the campfire experience without the actual fire.

CHAPTER 8:
EASY, BREEZY BEVERAGES

Chapter 8: Easy, Breezy Beverages

INSTANT GREEN SMOOTHIE

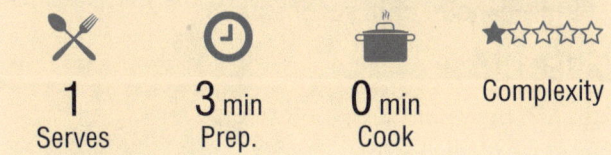

| 1 Serves | 3 min Prep. | 0 min Cook | Complexity |

INGREDIENTS
- 1 banana
- 1 cup spinach
- 1/2 cup almond milk
- 1 tablespoon honey
- 1/2 cup ice cubes

DIRECTIONS
Add all ingredients to a blender. Blend until smooth.

NUTRITIONAL INFORMATION: 130 calories | 2g protein | 25g carbs | 3g fat | 3g fiber | 0mg cholesterol | 100mg sodium | 400mg potassium.

QUICK TIP: The quickest way to get your veggies without eating them.

2-MINUTE LEMONADE

| 4 Serves | 2 min Prep. | 0 min Cook | Complexity |

INGREDIENTS
- 1 cup lemon juice
- 1 cup sugar
- 4 cups cold water

DIRECTIONS
Stir together lemon juice and sugar until the sugar dissolves.
Add water and stir.

NUTRITIONAL INFORMATION: 120 calories | 0g protein | 30g carbs | 0g fat | 0g fiber | 0mg cholesterol | 5mg sodium | 10mg potassium.

QUICK TIP: Add a splash of vodka for an adult version.

MINTY MEDITERRANEAN ICED GREEN TEA

4 Serves | **5 min** Prep. | **5 min** Cook* | Complexity

* (steeping)

INGREDIENTS
- 4 green tea bags
- 4 cups boiling water
- Fresh mint leaves (10-12 leaves)
- 1 lemon, thinly sliced
- Honey or agave syrup (optional)

DIRECTIONS
Place the tea bags and fresh mint leaves in a heat-proof pitcher.
Pour boiling water over them and let steep for 5 minutes.
Remove the tea bags and mint, then allow the tea to cool.
Once cooled, add the lemon slices and refrigerate until cold.
Serve over ice, adding sweetener if desired.

NUTRITIONAL INFORMATION: 0 calories | 0g protein | 0g carbs | 0g fat | 0g fiber | 0mg cholesterol | 0mg sodium | 10mg potassium.

QUICK TIP: Mint is a refreshing herb that provides an aromatic experience but also aids in digestion. Pairing with green tea amplifies the health benefits.

5-INGREDIENT SMOOTHIE

1 Serves | **3 min** Prep. | **0 min** Cook | Complexity

INGREDIENTS
- 1 cup frozen berries
- 1/2 banana
- 1/2 cup yogurt
- 1/2 cup orange juice
- 1 tablespoon chia seeds

DIRECTIONS
Add all ingredients to a blender. Blend until smooth.

NUTRITIONAL INFORMATION: 200 calories | 4g protein | 35g carbs | 4g fat | 5g fiber | 5mg cholesterol | 40mg sodium | 300mg potassium.

QUICK TIP: In a hurry? This smoothie is quicker to make than your morning coffee!

Chapter 8: Easy, Breezy Beverages

INSTANT CHAI LATTE

1 Serves | **2** min Prep. | **1** min Cook* | Complexity

*(microwave)

INGREDIENTS
- 1 chai tea bag
- 1 cup water
- 1 tablespoon honey
- 1/4 cup milk
- Cinnamon for garnish

DIRECTIONS
Microwave water for 1 minute and steep chai tea bag for 2-3 minutes.
Remove the tea bag, add honey and milk, and stir. Garnish with a sprinkle of cinnamon.

NUTRITIONAL INFORMATION: 100 calories | 1g protein | 20g carbs | 1g fat | 0g fiber | 5mg cholesterol | 15mg sodium | 50mg potassium.

QUICK TIP: If you can't visit your local coffee shop, bring the coffee shop to you—in less than 5 minutes!

QUICK DETOX WATER

4 Serves | **5** min Prep. | **0** min Cook | Complexity

INGREDIENTS
- 1 lemon, sliced
- 1 cucumber, sliced
- 1 mint sprig
- 4 cups of water

DIRECTIONS
Combine all ingredients in a large pitcher. Chill for at least 30 minutes before serving.

NUTRITIONAL INFORMATION: 5 calories | 0g protein | 1g carbs | 0g fat | 0g fiber | 0mg cholesterol | 0mg sodium | 10mg potassium.

QUICK TIP: Detox water: for when you've had a «detox-worthy» kind of day.

5-MINUTE GOLDEN MILK

1 Serves | 2 min Prep. | 3 min Cook* | Complexity

* (stove)

INGREDIENTS
- 1 cup milk (any type)
- 1 teaspoon turmeric
- 1/2 teaspoon cinnamon
- 1 tablespoon honey

DIRECTIONS
Heat milk on the stove.
Stir in turmeric, cinnamon, and honey.
Pour into a cup and enjoy!

NUTRITIONAL INFORMATION: 100 calories | 4g protein | 20g carbs | 1g fat | 0g fiber | 5mg cholesterol | 50mg sodium | 100mg potassium.

QUICK TIP: Golden milk, also known as «liquid gold,» is easier to make than finding a pot of gold at the end of a rainbow.

FAST BERRY INFUSED WATER

4 Serves | 5 min Prep. | 0 min Cook | Complexity

INGREDIENTS
- 1 cup mixed berries (strawberries, blueberries, raspberries)
- 4 cups water

DIRECTIONS
Place the berries in a pitcher.
Fill with water and refrigerate for 30 minutes to 1 hour before serving.

NUTRITIONAL INFORMATION: 10 calories | 0g protein | 2g carbs | 0g fat | 1g fiber | 0mg cholesterol | 0mg sodium | 10mg potassium.

QUICK TIP: Infused water counts as a serving of fruit, right? Asking for a friend.

DATE-INFUSED MEDITERRANEAN COFFEE

2 Serves | **10 min** Prep. | **5 min** Cook | Complexity ★★☆☆☆

INGREDIENTS
- 2 cups freshly brewed coffee
- 4-5 Medjool dates, pitted and chopped
- 1/4 teaspoon ground cardamom
- A pinch of salt
- Cream or milk (optional)

DIRECTIONS
Brew your coffee as usual.
Add the chopped dates while the coffee is still hot and let them steep for about 5 minutes.
Stir in the ground cardamom and a pinch of salt.
Allow the mixture to cool slightly before using a blender to process the variety until smooth and creamy.
Pour into cups and add cream or milk if desired.

NUTRITIONAL INFORMATION: 90 calories | 1g protein | 22g carbs | 0g fat | 2g fiber | 0mg cholesterol | 10mg sodium | 200mg potassium.

QUICK TIP: Dates, a staple in Mediterranean and Middle Eastern diets, are natural sweeteners. They add a touch of sweetness without the need for processed sugars, giving your coffee a delightful caramel note.

INSTANT HOT COCOA MIX

4 Serves | **2 min** Prep. | **2 min** Cook* | Complexity ★☆☆☆☆

* (microwave)

INGREDIENTS
- 1/2 cup cocoa powder
- 1/2 cup sugar
- A pinch of salt (optional)
- 4 cups milk (or water for a dairy-free version)
- Mini marshmallows (optional)

DIRECTIONS
In a bowl, mix cocoa powder, sugar, and salt.
Heat 1 cup of milk (or water) in the microwave for 1–2 minutes.
Add 2–3 tablespoons of the cocoa mix to the hot milk and stir until fully dissolved.
Top with mini marshmallows if desired.

NUTRITIONAL INFORMATION: 200 calories | 8g protein | 32g carbs | 4g fat | 3g fiber | 20mg cholesterol | 150mg sodium | 400mg potassium.

QUICK TIP: Keep a jar of the mixed dry ingredients on your counter. That way, you're always one step closer to cocoa bliss!

CHAPTER 9:
30-DAY MEAL PLAN: YOUR ROADMAP TO CULINARY HAPPINESS

QUICK TIP: Use the weekends to prep for the week ahead. Make bigger batches of recipes like dips, salads, and overnight oats throughout the week.

Chapter 9: 30-Day Meal Plan: Your Roadmap to Culinary Happiness

Day	Breakfast	Lunch	Dinner	Snack
1	Overnight Oats: Assemble & Forget	Turkey & Avocado Wrap	One-Pot Mediterranean Chicken	Instant Hummus & Veggies
2	Avocado & Tomato Toast	10-Minute Chicken Caesar Salad	Easy Baked Salmon	Quick Trail Mix
3	Microwave Veggie Omelet	Chickpea & Spinach Curry	Fast Vegetable Curry	No-Bake Energy Balls
4	Greek Yogurt with Honey & Walnuts	Instant Ramen Hack	Lemon Garlic Shrimp Pasta	Speedy Veggie Chips
5	5-Minute Smoothie Bowl	Lentil & Veggie Salad	Instant Pot Pulled Pork	Fruit & Nut Bars
6	Quick Breakfast Tacos	Veggie & Quinoa Bowl	15-Minute Fish Tacos	Olive & Cheese Skewers
7	Banana Pancakes: Flip & Fly	Express Chicken Quesadilla	5-Ingredient Black Bean Soup	Easy Veggie Spring Rolls
8	Quick & Filling Smoothie	Flash Veggie Stir-Fry	Quick Chicken Alfredo	Cheese & Cracker Bites
9	Quinoa Porridge	Speedy Spaghetti *Aglio e Olio*	Speedy Sheet Pan Fajitas	Protein-Packed Nut Mix
10	Muffin-tin Egg Bites	Spicy Tuna Salad	5-Ingredient Margherita Pizza	Quick Rice Cake Toppings
11	Breakfast Quesadilla	15-Minute Beef Stir-Fry	Quick Cauliflower Fried Rice	5-Minute Salsa & Chips
12	Instant Chia Pudding	Veggie & Quinoa Bowl	Speedy Sweet & Sour Chicken	Roasted Chickpeas
13	Bagel with Smoked Salmon	Instant Pot Chicken Risotto	Quick Greek Gyros	Mini Veggie Wraps
14	Speedy Shakshuka	Fast Falafel Wrap	Easy Lemon Herb Chicken	Olive & Cheese Skewers
15	Speedy Shakshuka	Quick Shrimp Tacos	One-Pot Mediterranean Chicken	Quick Trail Mix

Day	Breakfast	Lunch	Dinner	Snack
16	Instant Chia Pudding	Veggie & Quinoa Bowl	Instant Pot Pulled Pork	Easy Veggie Spring Rolls
17	Quinoa Porridge	15-Minute Beef Stir-Fry	Quick Greek Gyros	Quick Rice Cake Toppings
18	Banana Pancakes: Flip & Fly	Express Chicken Quesadilla	Easy Lemon Herb Chicken	Cucumber & Tuna Bites
19	Bagel with Smoked Salmon	Speedy Spaghetti *Aglio e Olio*	Quick Cauliflower Fried Rice	Instant Hummus & Veggies
20	Avocado & Tomato Toast	Instant Pot Chicken Risotto	Express Beef Stroganoff	Roasted Chickpeas
21	Breakfast Quesadilla	Flash Veggie Stir-Fry	15-Minute Fish Tacos	5-Minute Salsa & Chips
22	5-Minute Smoothie Bowl	Turkey & Avocado Wrap	Fast Vegetable Curry	Olive & Cheese Skewers
23	Microwave Veggie Omelet	Chickpea & Spinach Curry	20-Minute Beef & Broccoli	Fruit & Nut Bars
24	Greek Yogurt with Honey & Walnuts	10-Minute Chicken Caesar Salad	Speedy Sweet & Sour Chicken	Speedy Veggie Chips
25	Overnight Oats: Assemble & Forget	Spicy Tuna Salad	Lemon Garlic Shrimp Pasta	No-Bake Energy Balls
26	Zucchini & Egg Breakfast Wrap	Quick BBQ Chicken Pizza	Speedy Sheet Pan Fajitas	Cheese & Cracker Bites
27	Muffin-tin Egg Bites	Lentil & Veggie Salad	Easy Baked Salmon	Protein-Packed Nut Mix
28	Quick & Filling Smoothies	Instant Ramen Hack	Quick Chicken Alfredo	Mini Veggie Wraps
29	Instant Chia Pudding	Speedy Veggie Stir-Fry	15-Minute Beef Stir-Fry	Instant Hummus & Veggies
30	Quinoa Porridge	Turkey & Avocado Wrap	Quick Greek Gyros	Quick Trail Mix

CHAPTER 10:
FAQ AND SAVVY TIPS: NO, YOU CAN'T REPLACE OLIVE OIL WITH MOTOR OIL

Hello there, aspiring Mediterranean maestro! You've got the recipes, and the 30-day meal plan, and you're ready to rule your kitchen. I know you have questions. Worry not; we've got answers—and a dash of humor to boot.

Q1: CAN I SUBSTITUTE INGREDIENTS IF I DON'T HAVE WHAT THE RECIPE CALLS FOR?

A: Absolutely! You can swap similar ingredients like spinach for kale or brown rice for quinoa.

Q2: WHY SO MANY QUICK RECIPES? ARE WE RACING AGAINST THE CLOCK?

A: Because you've got a life outside of the kitchen! Whether running errands or binge-watching a TV series, quick recipes let you maintain a balanced diet without feeling chained to the stove.

Q3: HOW DO I KEEP MY FRESH VEGGIES FROM TURNING INTO SCIENCE EXPERIMENTS IN THE FRIDGE?

A: Plan your meals and shop accordingly. And if you find a stray veggie or two, our Flash Veggie Stir-Fry is a great last-minute rescue plan!

Q4: IS THERE SUCH A THING AS «TOO MUCH HUMMUS»?

A: In the Mediterranean Diet, the limit does not exist! Just remember, moderation is key.

Q5: WHY THE OBSESSION WITH OLIVE OIL?

A: It's the jack-of-all-trades in Mediterranean cooking. Use it for sautéing, dressing, or even as a dip—it's liquid gold!

Q6: WHAT IF I HAVE FOOD ALLERGIES?

A: Always check the ingredient list and adjust as needed. For example, seeds might be a good substitute in most recipes if you're allergic to nuts.

Q7: ANY TIPS FOR COOKING FISH?

A: Stick to our easy fish recipes, and remember: when cooking fish, less is often more.

Q8: CAN I EAT DESSERT AND STILL STICK TO THE MEDITERRANEAN DIET?

A: You bet! Our dessert section offers lighter options to satisfy that sweet tooth.

Q9: WHY SO MUCH GREEN STUFF?

A: Consider it «nature's confetti»—it adds color, flavor, and nutrients to your plate!

Q10: WHAT ABOUT ADJUSTING PORTION SIZES?

A: Most recipes are geared for 2-4 servings but can be easily doubled or halved. Just adjust the ingredient quantities accordingly.

Q11: WHAT IF I DON'T LIKE QUINOA?

A: No quin-woes! Feel free to replace it with rice, couscous, or cauliflower rice.

Q12: WHAT'S THE BEST RECIPE TO START WITH IF I'M NEW TO THE MEDITERRANEAN DIET?

A: Why not begin with our 5-Ingredient Black Bean Soup? It's easy, quick, and packs a flavor punch!

Q13: HOW CAN I STORE LEFTOVERS?

A: You can generally store most recipes in an airtight container in the fridge for 2-3 days. Some can even be frozen and reheated!

Q14: ANY COOKWARE RECOMMENDATIONS?

A: A good non-stick skillet and a sturdy chef's knife can go a long way. Invest in an Instant Pot for even quicker meal prep if you're keen.

Q15: I'VE TRIED 5-INGREDIENT SMOOTHIES, WHAT'S NEXT?

A: The sky's the limit! How about our Fast Berry Infused Water or 5-Minute Golden Milk? Variety is the spice of life!

And there you have it! Still curious? Email me, and I'll get back to you faster than you can say «Instant Pot Chili.» Happy cooking!

To make your culinary journey even more seamless, we've compiled some helpful resources that can act as your trusty kitchen companions. After all, cooking is more than just following recipes — it's about being well-informed and prepared.

MEASUREMENT CONVERSION CHART

Math might not have been your favorite subject in school. But a pinch of precision can make the difference between a masterpiece and a mishap when you're in the kitchen. To help you out, here's a quick measurement conversion chart for standard units:

Liquid Measurements

U.S. Measurement	Metric Conversion
1 cup	240 ml
1 pint (2 cups)	475 ml
1 quart (4 cups)	950 ml
1 gallon (16 cups)	3.8 L

Dry Measurements

U.S. Measurement	Metric Conversion
1 ounce	28 g
1 pound	454 g
1 teaspoon	5 ml
1 tablespoon	15 ml

Oven Temperatures

U.S. Measurement	Metric Conversion
250°F	120°C
300°F	150°C
350°F	175°C
400°F	200°C
450°F	230°C

Common Kitchen Measurements

U.S. Measurement	Metric Conversion
1 tablespoon	3 teaspoons
1 cup	16 tablespoons
1 pint	2 cups
1 quart	2 pints
1 gallon	4 quarts

Approximation	Equivalent
A pinch	~1/16 teaspoon

Approximation	Equivalent
A dash	~1/8 teaspoon

GLOSSARY FOR BEGINNERS

AGLIO E OLIO: Italian for «garlic and oil.» Elevate your pasta game with this simple but fancy-sounding treat. If it sounds posh, that's because it is.

AVOCADO: Nature's butter in a shell. Avocados are like the surprise in a cereal box, sometimes perfect, sometimes... just why?

BAGEL: New York's gift to breakfast. It's best served with smoked salmon unless you want a NY vs. Montreal debate.

BRUSCHETTA: When tomatoes decided to sit on toast and call it gourmet. Say «broo-SKET-tah» to sound fancy.

CHIA PUDDING: Tiny seeds that turn into breakfast magic with patience. Like overnight oats' more exotic cousin.

FALAFEL: Deep-fried chickpea balls. This is the best answer to any «I'm craving something crispy» moment.

GREEK YOGURT: Unlike the regular kind, it has a thick texture and a dash of boldness. Drizzle a little honey and sail away to a Greek island.

GYROS: Greek wraps that some people pronounce «YEE-ros» and others pronounce «JAI-ros.» Either way, they're delicious.

HUMMUS: Chickpeas that blended into stardom. Forget the store-bought version; homemade is where the heart (and taste) is.

OVERNIGHT OATS: The «set it and forget it» of breakfasts for those who want to eat fancy with zero AM effort.

PESTO: Basil's chance to shine. It goes well with almost anything, but watch for the garlic breath.

SHAKSHUKA: Eggs gently poached in a spicy tomato sauce. Perfect for those days when you want breakfast to pack a punch.

SHEET PAN FAJITAS: When you want to wrap up your day, literally. Get it? Because fajitas come in wraps?

TIRAMISU: This Italian sweet treat is rolled into both your caffeine fix and dessert craving. Who says you can't have your coffee and eat it too?

VEGGIE STIR-FRY: The quickest way to feel like you're doing right with vegetables. A colorful canvas of crunch and flavor.

ADDITIONAL RESOURCES

KITCHEN TOOLS GUIDE

For those moments when you wonder, «Do I really need this gadget?»

CHEF'S KNIFE: Your trusty sidekick. Makes dicing, chopping, and culinary magic possible.

CUTTING BOARD: The stage for all your ingredients. Remember, wooden for veggies and fruits, plastic for meats!

MEASURING CUPS & SPOONS: Because «eyeballing it» is for the brave and reckless.

BLENDER OR FOOD PROCESSOR: This tool is the magic behind the curtain, from smoothies to hummus.

NON-STICK SKILLET: Essential for those Shakshukas and Quick Chicken Alfredos. Less oil, less stick, more deliciousness.

MICROWAVE: More than just reheating leftovers. Hello, Microwave Veggie Omelet!

INSTANT POT: For when patience isn't your strong suit.

BONUS: MUFFIN TIN: Not just for muffins! Think Egg Bites and mini cheesecakes.

ESSENTIAL PANTRY ITEMS

The backbone of your Mediterranean culinary adventures.

OLIVE OIL: The heart and soul of Mediterranean cooking.

LENTILS & CHICKPEAS: Your protein-packed pals.

WHOLE GRAINS: Quinoa, bulgur, and whole grain pasta.

SPICES: Basil, oregano, cardamom, and more for those bursts of flavor.

NUTS: Walnuts, almonds, and pine nuts for that crunchy touch.

HONEY: For that natural sweet touch.

CANNED TOMATOES: Shakshukas, sauces, and so much more.

PAIRING SUGGESTIONS

Turn your meal from «Yum!» to «Is this a five-star restaurant?»

CHAPTER 1: QUICK BREAKFAST FIXES
Overnight Oats: Pair with a cold brew coffee and a fresh fruit salad to start your day.
Quick Breakfast Tacos: A homemade pico de gallo and a glass of orange juice.
Greek Yogurt with Honey & Walnuts: Enjoy with a side of mixed berries and herbal tea.

CHAPTER 2: BITE-SIZE SNACKS FOR THOSE MICRO-BREAKS
Instant Hummus & Veggies: Pair with a chilled white wine like a Sauvignon Blanc.
No-Bake Energy Balls: Enjoy with cold milk or a coffee.
Speedy Veggie Chips: Pair with a dipping sauce like ranch or a light beer.

CHAPTER 3: DIPS AND SIDES TO JAZZ UP YOUR MAIN COURSE
Whipped Feta: Pairs well with warm pita bread and a glass of Greek wine.
Quick & Zesty Salsa: Enjoy with tortilla chips and a cold lager.
Fast Lemon Garlic Asparagus: A perfect side for grilled meats and a glass of Chardonnay.

CHAPTER 4: LIGHTNING-FAST LUNCHES FOR THE OFFICE OR HOME
Turkey & Avocado Wrap: A side of sweet potato chips and a light iced tea.
Quick BBQ Chicken Pizza: Pair with a green salad, light beer, or soda.
15-Minute Beef Stir-Fry: A steamed rice and a glass of red wine like a Merlot.

CHAPTER 5: SPEEDY DINNERS: SO YOU CAN GET ON WITH YOUR EVENING
One-Pot Mediterranean Chicken: Enjoy with crusty bread and a glass of dry white wine.
Easy Baked Salmon: Pair with garlic-roasted asparagus and chilled Chardonnay.
Quick Cauliflower Fried Rice: A cold lager beer and additional soy or teriyaki sauce for dipping.

CHAPTER 6: 5-INGREDIENT WONDERS
5-Ingredient Black Bean Soup: A cornbread and a simple salad with vinaigrette.
5-Ingredient Pasta Carbonara: A side of garlic bread and a glass of Italian red wine like Chianti.

CHAPTER 7: SATISFY THAT SWEET TOOTH IN MINUTES
Quick Berry Sorbet: Serve with a sprig of fresh mint and a glass of dessert wine.

5-Minute Brownies: Pair with a scoop of vanilla ice cream and a glass of cold milk.

Quickie Chocolate Fondue: Serve with strawberries, bananas, and a glass of wine or champagne.

CHAPTER 8: EASY, BREEZY BEVERAGES

Instant Green Smoothie: Perfect with a light breakfast like toast and fruit.

2-Minute Lemonade: Great with a sandwich or a light salad.

Instant Hot Cocoa Mix: Enjoy with a side of cookies or brownies for a sweet treat.

INGREDIENT SUBSTITUTIONS

Because sometimes you can't find «that one ingredient».

GREEK YOGURT: Can't find it? Regular yogurt strained through a cheesecloth can be a makeshift substitute.

QUINOA: Bulgur or couscous can be a replacement.

OLIVE TAPENADE: No olives? Try a mix of capers and sun-dried tomatoes.

CHIA SEEDS (FOR PUDDING): Ground flax seeds can give a similar texture.

SHAKSHUKA'S SPICES: Can't find the exact spice? A bit of cumin, paprika, and chili powder can work wonders.

Remember, cooking is as much about improvisation as it is about precision. Sometimes, the best dishes come from a bit of culinary jazz!

INDEX

Avocado & Tomato Toast 12

Bagel with Smoked Salmon.....................15
Banana Pancakes: Flip & Fly..................16
Beef & Broccoli, 20-Minute.....................47
Beef & Rice, 5-Ingredient 58
Beef Stroganoff, Expres...........................53
Beef Stir-Fry, 15-Minute..........................40
Berry Infused Water 74
Berry Sorbet..62
Black Bean Soup, 5-Ingredient...............56
Bruschetta, Tomato & Basil...................29
Brownies, 5-Minute.................................64

Caesar Salad, 10-Minute Chicken 36
Carbonara, 5-Ingredient Pasta...............57
Cauliflower Fried Rice, Quick.................52
Cheesecake Cups, No-Bake 64
Cheese & Cracker Bites...........................19
Chickpea & Spinach Curry......................37
Chicken Alfredo, Quick...........................50
Chicken Caesar Salad, 10-Minute 36
Chicken Quesadilla, Express 44
Chicken Risotto, Instant Pot 42
Chicken Stir-Fry, 5-Ingredient 57
Choco-Mousse, Instant............................63
Chia Pudding, Instant..............................15
Cookies, 3-Ingredient...............................62
Coleslaw, Quick 33
Corn Salad, Fresh 31
Curry, Fast Vegetable 48

Date-Infused Mediterranean Coffee 75
Detox Water, Quick 73

Egg Bites, Muffin-tin 14
Egg Breakfast Wrap, Zucchini................17
Egg Fried Rice, 5-Ingredient 59
Energy Balls, No-Bake.............................20

Falafel Wrap, Fast....................................44
Fish & Chips, 5-Ingredient 59
Fish Tacos, 15-Minute 51
Flash Veggie Stir-Fry................................37
Flash-Pickled Veggies..............................31
Fondue, Quickie Chocolate.....................67
Fried Rice, Quick Cauliflower.................52
Fruit & Nut Bars 22
Fruit Salad, Speedy..................................63
Fajitas, Speedy Sheet Pan.......................50

Golden Milk, 5-Minute 74
Greek Gyros, Quick..................................54
Greek Yogurt with Honey & Walnuts.....11
Guacamole, 5-Minute 27

Hot Cocoa Mix, Instant 75
Hummus & Veggies, Instant 19

Iced Green Tea, Minty Mediterranean....72
Instant Pot
    Chili 47
    Pulled Pork 51
Instant Ramen Hack................................39

Lemon Bars, Fast & Easy........................65
Lemon Garlic Asparagus, Fast 33
Lemon Garlic Shrimp Pasta 49
Lemon Herb Chicken, Easy 52
Lemonade, 2-Minute 71
Lentil & Veggie Salad...............................41

Margherita Pizza, 5-Ingredient 56
Mediterranean Chicken, One-Pot 46
Mini Veggie Wraps 23
Mint Salad, Cucumber.............................34
Muffin-tin Egg Bites 14

No-Bake:
    Cheesecake Cups 64
    Energy Balls...20
    Oat Cookies..67

Olive & Cheese Skewers..........................23
Olive Tapenade 29
Overnight Oats: Assemble & Forget........10

Pancakes, Banana: Flip & Fly.................16
Pancakes, 5-Ingredient............................60
Pesto, Instant...28
Pickled Veggies, Flash 31
Pizza
    BBQ Chicken, Quick...........................38
    Margherita, 5-Ingredient 56
Pulled Pork, Instant Pot 51

Quesadilla, Breakfast...............................14
Quesadilla, Express Chicken 44
Quinoa:
    Porridge..13

Salad, Easy..32
Bowl, Veggie 40

Ramen Hack, Instant...............................39
Red Pepper Dip, Roasted 32
Rice:
Cake Toppings, Quick 22
Fried Rice, Quick Cauliflower 52
Pudding, 10-Minute 66
Risotto, Instant Pot Chicken 42
Roasted:
Chickpeas..21
Red Pepper Dip 32

Salad
Caesar, 10-Minute Chicken...............36
Coleslaw, Quick 33
Corn, Fresh 31
Lentil & Veggie 41
Tuna, Spicy 38
Salsa
& Chips, 5-Minute 24
Quick & Zesty 30
Shakshuka, Speedy..................................13
Sheet Pan Fajitas, Speedy........................50
Shrimp
Pasta, Lemon Garlic 49
Tacos, Quick 43
Skewers, Olive & Cheese........................23
Smoothies
Bowl, 5-Minute..................................10
Pops, Instant 25
Green, Instant 71
Quick & Filling..................................16
5-Ingredient.......................................72
Snacks, Bite-Size......................................18
Sorbet, Quick Berry 62
Soup, 5-Ingredient Black Bean...............56
Spaghetti Aglio e Olio, Speedy 39
Speedy Dinners..45
Spinach Curry, Chickpea........................37
Spring Rolls, Easy Veggie........................25
Stir-Fry
Beef, 15-Minute 40
Flash Veggie 37

Veggie, Flash 37
Stroganoff, Express Beef 53
Sweet & Sour Chicken, Speedy................53
Sweet Tooth in Minutes...........................61

Tacos
Breakfast, Quick 11
Fish, 15-Minute 51
Shrimp, Quick 43
Veggie, 5-Ingredient..........................58
Tapenade, Olive 29
Tiramisu Cups, Speedy............................68
Tomato
& Basil Bruschetta.............................29
Basil Soup, 5-Ingredient 60
Toast, Avocado 12
Trail Mix, Quick.......................................20
Tuna Bites, Cucumber 24
Tuna Salad, Spicy 88
Turkey & Avocado Wrap.........................36

Veggie
Bowl, Veggie & Quinoa......................40
Chips, Speedy 21
Salad, Lentil..41
Stir-Fry, Flash 37
Tacos, 5-Ingredient 58
Wraps, Mini..23
Veggie Stir-Fry, Speedy 30

Whipped Feta 27
Wraps
Breakfast Wrap, Zucchini & Egg........17
Turkey & Avocado 36

Yogurt
Sauce, Garlic.......................................28
with Honey & Walnuts, Greek 11
Frozen, Instant 66

Zucchini
& Egg Breakfast Wrap.......................17
Chips, Speedy Veggie 21

Made in the USA
Columbia, SC
29 September 2024